From The Collection: JoAnn

A Tribute Dedication to All Who Hope and Dream,
Have Lived and Felt the Loss and Fully Appreciate,
and, the Many Who May Want to Believe in Love

by Ray M. Helstrom

DORRANCE
PUBLISHING CO
EST. 1920
PITTSBURGH, PENNSYLVANIA 15238

Dorrance Publishing Co
585 Alpha Drive
Pittsburgh, PA 15238
Visit our website at *www.dorrancebookstore.com*

ISBN: 978-1-4809-5712-1
eISBN: 978-1-4809-5735-0

Dedication

To the positive forces and good people who most influenced my life. Particularly my family: Parents Verne and Dorothy, sister Carolyn, brothers Lyle, Bruce and Thomas, and son Marek, and June, and of course JoAnn.

Acknowledgments

Thank you to my close friends, many teachers and colleagues over these many years. A necessary thank you to my supportive family: Marek, Wendy and Darlene, Carolyn and Spence, and Donna, and to my very supportive friends who provided so much in my time of need: John, Nell and Madelyn, and Betty, and Ann, and a very special nod to JoAnn's Father and Mother, brother Eugene and Nancy, and in-law sons Gregory and Douglas, and so many who were very close to JoAnn; Ann, Boots, Gerry, Marie, Margaret, Cindy, Shirley, and all of the Alumni of Kwajalein/USAKA and OLLI/UAH, and members of University Baptist Church, Huntsville friends, and Willow Springs neighbors.

Disclaimers

The "JoAnn" book is a collection of non-researched remembrances written as anecdotes that are primarily true, though general as to actual time. Any person identified with a surname is mentioned for the personal service they rendered. All given names may have been altered to "protect" the innocent and guilty.

Any and all errors are mine. All musical lyrics have been paraphrased and acknowledged. The ending initials and dates identify the work as mine with an approximate date of creation.

Ray M. Helstrom

Contents

Introduction

What you see and do will become your memories.
I was made aware of this reality when I became involved and immersed in writing anecdotes about incidents in my life as therapy to abate the possibility of any onslaught of severe grief due to the loss of my wife to ovarian cancer. For me, it was a wise option.

Like most, my daily functions are performed by an assortment of habits, none of which offered much beyond their normal practicality. The exercise of writing about dredged up remembrances developed into a sort of hobby, which over some six years amassed into a large variety of anecdotal comments.

The receipt of a kind comment from my cousin Sue, suggesting that I should "share" some of my written recollections with others touched me rather sharply, somewhat like a spur. Over the years, there had been other positive reactions from an abundance of other family members and close friends, all of which I gratefully accepted as flattering comments. Some had even suggested publishing, which was beyond my comprehension.

It was the concept of sharing, a rather rare element in my lexicon, that urged the undertaking of the effort that led to the creation of what I intend to be a "three-little-book" trilogy collection keepsake.

The hope is that these small "booklets" may provide a chuckle to the reader, and, as random thought recordings, also serve to stir the senses of others in a manner that triggers similar personal memories. In doing so, they would provide a purpose far beyond what they dutifully did for me.

These booklets are not biographical stories. They are compilations of brief anecdotes collected and somewhat chronologically arranged within a titled theme. For color and flavor, the principle element within each story has been accented with other random recollections. To expand the narrative, major segments within a theme have been augmented with related photographs.

"From the Collection <> JoAnn" might be classified as a romance literature effort expressed in the memoir genre. In musical terms, it might be likened to a serenade; "a work in several movements that is freer in expression, intended for casual entertainment". Hopefully you enjoy the experiment.

Ray M. Helstrom

Seeing Her

To be painfully honest, when writing, I find that my efforts to convey the meaning of a matter or create an adequate description of a subject are severely limited by the shallowness of my ability. However, to be perfectly frank, I also write with total unconcern. My hope is that even though some anecdotes may be deeply mined, they will actually be easy to absorb or swallow, depending on the story.

A good example is this effort to convey my inner image of JoAnn after being without her in my life over the past seven years. I have photographs, of course. Thankfully in considerable quantity, and, even more important, equally great in variety as to aspects of time, composition and place.

To describe JoAnn is beyond my capability. I do remember that my first sighting of her registered in a manner that happened only 2 or 3 times in my life. I somewhat recall the precise locations that I first saw her, and then upon occasion, again and again, but I can't say with certainty. The uniqueness of our place and nature of community had a bearing on the totality of it all. Our acquaintanceship was not sudden. Acceptance by others was important. After actually meeting, I recall that we blended well and without any real disruption our involvement seemed to marinate into a compatible togetherness.

JoAnn was very personable, whatever that may convey. She was outgoing, enthusiastic, energetic, accommodating, curious, sweet, very proper, and with her forgiveness, she reeked of goodness. Along with a certain flair, she was beautiful and fun to be around.

Over the generous span of my life, several activities have transpired in repeated spurts - playing golf, traveling, attending school, enjoying theater, and *seeing movies*. The latter is the easiest to do, and the earliest I did, which is probably why it's an impressionable source and why they readily serve as an available tool of assistance for me.

To convey a visual image of JoAnn, considering my limitations, I offer this cinematic composite:

The *'angelic glow'* of Sabrina – (Audrey Hepburn)

The *'innocence'* of GiGi – (Leslie Caron)

The *'spunk and size'* of Gidget – (Sally Field)

I could give or take a few others, but I'll settle for these. Besides, when I wish to conjure up a glimpse, I have the photos and feelings and not-too-deeply buried memories.

RMH

11-2016

Award Winner

When read by Donna, JoAnn's daughter, she replied, "Thank you for loving my mother."

Awestruck, I responded, "Thank you, the pleasure was mine."

Part I

The Beginning

South Seas

Introduction

Relationship

Somewhere In Time

Except that it happened to me, it may possibly have been just a routine man-meets-woman / man-gets-woman happenstance. But, to this somewhat hapless being, it was one of the grandest love affairs. Think Laura, Nellie, and Gigi, or, "*A Summer's Place*" and "*An Affair To Remember*". Throw in "*An American In Paris*" and "*Brigadoon*" and you begin to get a sense of it. Circumstances dictate that "*Tales of The South Pacific*" also deserves a cameo mention.

This may leave you with the impression that I'm a silly movie buff, or over-imaginative show business devotee, or some sort of simple wimp. I don't believe this is true. But then again, I do see myself as being timid, if not downright awkward in the presence of the gentler sex. However, in my defense, I hasten to say that my behavior has always been one of appreciation and respect, for which authentic ladies have always seemed to be accepting of me. My guess is that this was because I was non-threatening. I know this must be true because non-ladies, as best as I can recall, have never, ever, even deemed to acknowledge my presence.

I actually have no recollection of any past social encounter that could be described as being aggressive or even bold, at least on my part. Which is why, when I think back to our first dance, on the occasion of our first formal introduction, my first comment to JoAnn, which was, "It will be fabulous when we get together", came as a shock, even to me. She squirmed only slightly. She didn't terminate the dance, but there was no conversation either. I'd like to believe that she was thinking it over because, after we finished the dance, to my utter dismay, thereafter, both of our lives were on a redirected path.

Perhaps it's best to go back a few steps.

(To be continued)

How Sweet The Sound

Allow me the indulgence of telling you about what happened to this stranger in paradise. Others, too, may have had the elation of viewing a grand vista through two pair of eyes and seeing it as a single sight; of savoring each moment with the taste buds of two as they relish as one the joyous juice of life, or of being one of a couple so compatibly connected in sense and pulse as if to be possessed of one, fully-mated heart. If so, welcome.

Such shared intimacies are deserving of honorable gestures, thankful prayers, and an enduring gratitude. Verification lies in the abundance of testimony that is so richly chronicled in the name of love. Merely reference mankind's vast store of literature, song, and devoted performance of dedicated deeds for convincing confirmation. My song is but a single-sounded note within this cherished chorus.

I offer no guidance on how to seek true love. If you hold its treasured capability within you, guard and nurture it well so that at your appointed time it can serve you in turn. The aura of blossom and bloom it bestows upon one's life is beyond description. I simply submit this note of added testimonial assurance that, when your moment comes, you will be humbled, happy, and immeasurably glad. For me, her name was JoAnn.

On the one hand, one might think that the confines of a tiny crowded island, which offers little privacy or opportunity for seclusion, would have a dampening effect on a relationship. On the other, intentions are readily perceived. If one's pursuits are open and honest, such an environment can be truly nurturing. Proof in support of this latter theory comes from my having lived a closely shared experience in just such an island community.

When residing in an isolated, closed colony, it's the small things that hold sway in matters of meaning. Minor things become major. Everything you see, feel and do leaves a larger impression and becomes more indelible, and ever-enduring. As the area of living is contracted, and the full scope and range of life is diminished, every activity seems to gain in importance. Each shared experience is grander in moment and even greater in value. Dining is more intimate, dancing is more joyous, parties more festive, and swimming and snorkeling in a lagoon or merely sunning on a beach becomes even more expansive in terms of fun. The pace of knowing someone is rapidly advanced, and the ease of compatibility, without any personal awareness, quickly grows into a state of natural acceptance.

JoAnn and I were granted the chance to live as if we had all the time in the world. We never measured our time together in moments, but in entire days and nights sumptuously filled with laughter, joy and love. Our miracle of togetherness endured for over a quarter century. To this day I continue to ask, "How could this be?"

RMH
4-2012

Kwajalein – On Land

In a sense, or more likely in reality, when JoAnn and I ventured to Kwa-jalein Island we both had unknowingly embarked on "another" life. For her, perhaps a second or third; for me, most certainly my fourth or fifth. In terms of pathways and experience, of course.

JoAnn arrived first into a welcoming situation full of friends. Not that it wasn't extremely different, it was, but in several ways she would find her life to be favorably altered. It would become more liberated and vastly more stimulating compared to what she had ever known. She was immediately adopted into a familiar work environment among support-ive friends that provided camaraderie and security while offering her a change in responsibilities and a totally new and broader social network.

By definition, an island is land surrounded by water. The Marshall Is-lands are a large collection of several hundred small islands and atolls situated far off in the South Pacific Ocean. A small grouping of these are uniquely clustered to form an enclosed, triangular shaped, 60 miles long, 20-mile wide lagoon, the entirety of which is surrounded by the ocean. Only three navi-gable waterways offer entrance into the south area of this calm water lagoon.

The largest atoll in this group is located at the southernmost corner of the lagoon. It is shaped in the form of a 3-mile long, quarter-mile wide boomerang. This land area was designated, designed and developed as a "town/village" community that contains all of the functioning necessities for the vital needs and expectations of a society of active American families. At least up to the limitations of possibility when you consider the reality of it all. This is Kwajalein; the island setting for many life-altering stories. JoAnn's adventure is but one.

Though seemingly confining, restrictive, and limited as a lifestyle, which is true, there are other aspects worth considering. The first being, to not ignore the ingenuity of the "American Way". A second is the very non-or-limited costs associated with living an unusual, "off-shore", island way of life. Especially with the benefits of having a fully furnished and maintained place to dwell and access to a daily menu of ample and conveniently served edible meals that accompany an income tax advantage. And further, with all needs of transport satisfied with a bicycle and a tropical environment that dictates casual living, most of the costs of normal life are reduced to modest, at best.

In spite of the limitations of land and landscape, where a single road circles the land area, and the word luxury would never be applied to any of Kwajalein's amenities, the many facilities allocated to support and serve the needs of the community tended to lessen most essential concerns.

The island has an airport and scheduled flight operation; a full medical/dental service is available; children enjoy a K-12 school system; shopping needs are met by amply stocked department, sundry, beverage, and grocery stores; grooming needs and wishes are serviced by a beauty salon and full line laundry facility; and, though nighttime viewing is al fresco, movies are screened regularly, whether raining or not.

As elsewhere, the normal process of daily life on Kwajalein was dedicated to one's job assignment. A sense of feeling toward all personal time beyond this practicality would be similar to the lifestyle a normal family would experience on a lake shore resort vacation, with one proviso; living life on a small island demanded adjustments. Due to the serious necessity of maintaining one's sanity, and to preclude the climbing of palm trees, involvement in at least one activity of choice was "mandatory". To this end, an extensive, endless effort was devoted to satisfying the leisure time vacuum of everyone in the Kwajalein community. Over time the morale and recreation needs and wishes of a variety of high tech and all-trades workers, a sundry collection of males and females, and family members of all ages, have been applied, practiced and incorporated into the lifestyle of "Kwaj".

The tasks of the island exist for a serious purpose, which may best explain why daily life beyond duty was embraced at such an enthusiastic and energetic pace. Perhaps everyone was trying to maintain a balance to the stress of the mission. Then again, it could be that living a normal life in a far away, more distant, and less demanding way, simply allowed everyone to feel unfettered.

JoAnn immediately found the many amenities available for a truly active life to be not only convenient but stimulating and a lot of fun. The morale boosting facilities and opportunities offered on Kwajalein consisted of three levels of diversion and intensity:

The first cushion available to everyone were the personal, family and all purpose facilities: A chapel, a library, an assortment of meeting rooms and hobby workshops, a major beach and playground, swimming pools for families and bachelors, and bowling lanes. Children enjoyed school activities.

JoAnn invested time in chapel services, beach and pool sunbathing, and later developed a devoted interest in gardening. When she departed Kwajalein she reaped over $800 from the sale of her plants.

The second free time category met the recreational needs and demands for active participation beyond normal family affairs and community socializing activities.

The Command established a department of recreation within its Community Service division which provided a broad assortment of facilities and support for all manner of independent and organized sports involvement for all ages, desires, aptitudes and attitudes. Enthusiasm ran high. The only thing ever cautioned was temperament - an island community is too close knit for untoward behavior.

Impassioned, dedicated and serious participation was conducted continuously in the areas of:

Golf- with a nine-hole course and a club house

Softball – enjoyed a playing field with bleachers and ferocious competition

Tennis – had fenced courts and practice walls (also used for handball)

Basketball – had an outdoor court for pickup and team scheduled games

Scuba divers – had an operating facility with air tank and dive trip service, and not to be ignored were running, biking, wind surfing and the stellar activity of sailing.

JoAnn would profess to being non-athletic; however, she dabbled at golf, was involved in Scuba, and had friends in most sports, especially sailing. Much later she bravely tried snow skiing in Colorado.

A third category of free time diversion was akin to normal American life, with the exception that the close nature of island life dictated a far greater and more frequent inter-involvement with everyone. Somehow everyone was attached to someone or something; their company, a co-worker, a co-interest, or co-desire. No one was left out. The combining of home and communal social life was the way of life on Kwaj, which is probably the factor that best explains why their tour on Kwajalein has been so universally grand and momentous in memory to all of its alumni.

Along with the few private affairs conducted at billeted homes, the community at large was provided with a variety of facilities which were dedicated and continuously employed in the conduct of essential island affairs, all holiday celebrations, and any and every desired and imagined occasion that could be conceived for the purpose of general morale, enjoyment, happiness and mere fun.

Lasting remembrances were made at two primary sites: The Yukwe Yuk Club, where more formal and organized occasions were conducted, and the pavilion at Emon Beach, where the affairs were just as intense but more casual in dress. The two most popular events were the celebration of birthdays and farewells. A bit more selective in audience, and even more frequent in loyal patronage, were the Vets Hall and Yacht Club lagoon side and Local Boy ocean side pavilions.

In many ways, Kwajalein itself was a celebration, especially when things went well, as they most certainly did for JoAnn. She broadly participated in the lifestyle on the land of Kwaj and gratefully benefited from and enjoyed its largess. She especially reveled in the dinner dances and costume parties, and over time became adept in the role of hostess. She liked people and appreciated her many friends, which, with good fortune included myself. It was the communal spirit of Kwajalein that nurtured our relationship and in time fostered our marriage.

RMH

6-2015

A Good Day For Normals

At a time a long while back, when I landed on a Marshallese Island far off, deep in the South Pacific, Colonel John, Jr. was already entrenched in his assignment as Commander of the Army Missile Range on that same Kwajalein atoll. His task was of premier importance regarding both need and responsibility. The Kwajalein community was under a review that had determined that conditions were becoming too lax for the purpose of its mission.

Col. John found himself seated at an unusual table being served a full plate of unpalatable issues. His assignment had been greeted in a far different and more confrontational manner than normally experienced on Kwajalein. Due to the tremor of the community shake-up, the usual atmosphere of casual harmony was filled with drama and a great deal of anxiety.

My civilian contractor assignment several layers below Col. John's would best be described as being at the morale level. It involved doubling the size of the retail service facility so it held some importance and interest in the community. Having no work experience as to military projects, I was impressed and relieved by Col. John's business-like manner and approach to the proceedings. The remodel project was exceedingly successful and it came about that I was given the honor of accompanying Col. John at the ribbon cutting ceremony.

On a personal note, I had come to this unique situation semi-retired, unattached and in what I thought would be a short indulgence in an off-the-clock adventure. As circumstance would dictate, an attractive, petite, especially chaste Southern lady, in a life situation similar to mine, was also on the island. She was billeted in a civil service post assigned to the command office headquarters. The relationship between military and government overseer personnel and civilian contracted citizens was that a formal distance was to be maintained. As social life and human nature further dictated, a few months down the road she and I became discretely but more informally acquainted.

During this unpropitious time of community turmoil, possibly due to concerns regarding employment, one disturbed civilian citizen felt the need to forward a private anonymous letter to Commander Col. John objecting to the activities of a named government employee and myself, a civilian employee. This became an instant issue at the command level, which, as obviously intended, could result in the expulsion from the island of any distracting or disturbing element or person.

The named government career employee was summoned to Colonel John's office where upon he informed her that his office had received an accusatory letter using her name. Being a very proper and especially innocent person concerning unsavory situations, and now being suddenly thrust into a vulnerable and hideous position that seriously concerned her livelihood, she was especially astonished to then witness Col. John's actions and hear his next words: He tore up the letter, and said, "Piss on them, you and Ray do what you want."

Col. John, Jr. never gave the incident another thought. At that moment at least, he had too many and far heavier matters on his desk.

The consequences of Col. John's decision would be left to the future and in time would become our history. Neither he nor we - JoAnn, the command office secretary and me, Ray - had the slightest inkling of the impact his permission and counsel would have on the lives of two very normal, average, rather humble, meandering people.

What time and the future revealed for JoAnn and Ray as their lives unfolded over the next quarter century, in terms of a close relationship and enviable, jubilant lifestyle, turned out to be heaven sent.

The judicious permission granted by Col. John, Jr. on that fateful day manifested into a blessing far beyond what any of us could have ever dreamed or imagined.

Thank you, Colonel.

RMH
1-2014

(continued) Somewhere In Time

I had come to a strange, small island alone and on my own, having agreed to undertake an assignment to fix a problem. I had no awareness of the situation, no personal contacts, and no ambitions beyond what I understood to be a short-term contract to do what was needed.

Looking back, I approached the assignment much as one would eagerly and enthusiastically immerse themselves in a favorite hobby. The pursuit was successful to the tune of lasting over ten years. The accompanying idyllic lifestyle was an added perk.

The first time I saw JoAnn she was seated in a newly created section of the store trying on shoes. She was an attractive distraction during the activity of a busy day. Sometime later, I saw her again at the exit door, where I was standing for some reason. I even recall having said something arcane to her, such as, "Thank you for coming in."

My next remembrance was seeing her seated in the bleachers at the softball field. It was on a Sunday after a leisurely lunch. I had strolled over to take a look at the game that was under way. She was sitting alone. I quietly sat down in the space next to her. She may have been there to watch one of the players. If so, to this day, I don't know which one. There may have been other interests in her life. I simply never knew, never asked, nor ever cared a wit.

After a while, nonchalantly, we started to chat; what she did, where she worked, where she was from, and such. She was on island as a government employee assigned as a secretary in the commanding officer's office. Due to her good work efforts in her job at the Kwajalein Headquarters office on the Redstone Arsenal in Huntsville, Alabama, she had been offered this choice opportunity. Having raised three children as a divorced single mom, her family, as a just reward, had encouraged her to accept this chance at a personal adventure.

Our talk got a little deeper and came to a discussion as to a decision she was contemplating concerning traveling back to her home in Athens, Alabama to attend the wedding ceremony of her youngest son. This was a serious subject and momentous matter. My input was simple and sincere. If at all possible, she should go since such occasions were too important to miss. She went. It's not unreasonable to believe that perhaps this contributed to why I would become a factor in her life.

In time, due to the uniqueness of my job and the construction project, I came to mingle and know most of the movers-and-shakers on the island, the manager of the Yokwe Yuk dinner and social club being one of the closest. Frank and I had arrived on the island about the same time. When he decided to emphasize a happy hour occasion, he needed a part-time hostess to manage the activity. Without any input from me, he hired JoAnn, which didn't diminish the importance of the deed.

Though her extra "happy hour" part-time activity was briefly held, I believe she relished it, and it was this short span of time that presented a reason for our more formal encounter. It came about as a casual suggestion from her that I join her group to meet a recently-arrived new friend. I was pleased to accept. By now, you know where my interest was focused, and you now know how the stage was set for the why, where and when of our first dance.

The normal separation of overseer and performer was formalized under the status of a military contract. Yet, somehow, with JoAnn ensconced in the government/military community and myself involved in a high profile job as a member of the contractor/civilian community, our acquaintanceship continued to grow. This blended aspect of our work assignments actually granted us a mutual benefit. As a couple, we enjoyed entry into all levels and variety of island social activities. The broad acceptance and approval we received throughout the Kwajalein social community was truly supportive. Over time, I'm sure that this situation played a large and favorable role in the development of our transformation from being a "friendly us" into a more binding "committed we".

One occasion was especially momentous. At the close of another cordial evening with Gerry and Joe, a popular island couple, JoAnn and I were invited to their home to further partake of Gerry's hospitality. We talked long into the early morning as we reminisced over music from Joe's collection of records. At the very least, this occasion set the course of our togetherness to the point of acknowledging and designating Joe as the "godfather" of our relationship.

I believe that a few highlights from the "idyllic lifestyle list" we amassed during the time of living our enviable lives in this unusual location could serve to offer others a glimpse at what an extraordinary experience a shared life can be.

For now, I'll leave that for another time.

RMH

4-2011

Getting To Know You

As promised, I herein offer a few highlights of an idyllic existence in a unique location to serve as a glimpse of how rich the experience of a shared life can be.

After duty and dedication to one's job, a primary feature of life on Kwajalein was the hosting of, or attendance at, occasions, parties, celebrations, ceremonies, events and functions. These activities were held at the behest or dictate of' personal desires, corporate business or morale needs, command protocol, calendared holidays, and the constructive and social purposes of assorted groups and sports clubs, and, for the festive gatherings enthusiastically concocted by a large cadre of Hawaiian "local boys".

They were all good, for the good of all. Looking back, I wonder how we ever squeezed in time for participation in organized team sports, hobbies, sailing, and the obligations of faith and regular life. Somehow we did.

✦

By way of defining a beginning, I'd have to say that our mutual effort to compose a re-mindful theme for our first "castaway-on-a-south-seas-island" Christmas Season would be a fitting start. A large piece of ornament-adorned driftwood amusingly served as our symbolic tree. There were minor gifts and selected friends, an assortment of foods, and moderate toasts to hopes and wishes, some open and some silent. This was a propitious occasion that revealed the outward joy and inner sweetness of JoAnn. Thereafter, my every effort to cultivate our relationship was devoted to the nurturing of these endearing traits.

⁂

A madcap bonding episode concerning JoAnn and myself is worth mentioning. Being relatively new arrivals on island, our status had been classified as "bachelor", which dictated that our living quarters were best described as "cell-like". The event happened due to a common practice among those who occupied furnished houses and trailers. JoAnn was offered a house-sitting treat from friends who went off-Island on their annual holiday. She would have use of their furnished trailer during this allotted span of time.

We decided to turn this opportunity into our first social gesture as a couple. It was an attempt to return the favor of innumerable accepted invitations to others' hospitality. This event brought out the traits of cordiality and manners-under-duress that were naturally possessed by JoAnn. Both would be amply tested during a very small party event that turned into an unmanageable calamity.

It was from Jerry, a young man from New Jersey, who often boasted about his prowess as a master pizza maker where our often-repeated party theme was born. We made plans for a modest party featuring his pizzas; a date was set, provisions were stocked, word was spread.

It should be mentioned that the social mingling of oversight army and government personnel and contractor employees was not condoned. And also, that trailers are small. Tragically, in light of what transpired, the social rules of the island were severely strained and our minimal party space, with one small oven, proved to be woefully inadequate to service the occasion.

To critique the event, JoAnn was too popular and I was too enthusiastic. Our modest plan and plea for attendance was answered by a cast of seemingly hundreds from every rank and station, task and duty, and all sizes and shapes of humanity that were represented on the island. The response simulated a small riot. It was overwhelming, frightening, exhilarating and laughable.

It was all friendly, but Jerry was demolished. The evening was somewhat salvaged by enlisting the help of close friends who managed the island's dinner club and snack bar. JoAnn gallantly survived, but she instantly became known, not only as a nice person, but somewhat infamous.

⁕

While on the topic of parties, we thereafter continued to wedge our small efforts onto the island calendar. However, with lessons learned, we rotated them among our friends from various sets and groups, with only a few always included.

To illustrate the endearing innocence of JoAnn, I must introduce Nate. Along with Father O'Brian, he was a regular. He was one of only 3 or 4 black gentlemen on island. He was a tech photographer when I arrived, widely known, and well liked far beyond the fact that he often conducted free dance lessons. He later acquired the necessary licenses and became the captain of the island's large inter-island commuter/transport barge.

One evening, we held a great party, at a house, I believe, since there was a large crowd. JoAnn was in her full state of enthusiasm and revelry. One of her party "devices" was for each guest to have the name of a famous or known person stuck onto their backs when they arrived. During the course of the evening, guests were to ask other guests for clues as to who they were supposed to be. I don't know who concocted the names, but JoAnn joyously greeted arrivals and then plucked a name out of a bag and pasted it onto their backs.

At this event, Nate spent the whole night trying to determine who he was. He never found out until at the end of the evening, when, to good natured fun and uproarious laughter, he found out he was "Buckwheat".

Now, if you knew JoAnn, you would chuckle and understand why she was chagrined and would be thereafter for the rest of her life. You would know full well that she did not possess even an ounce of the devious wit necessary to ever perceive of such humor or, God forbid, potential for hurt. Her aversion to the possibility of harming anyone else was immutable. Even as an innocent act of joviality, such behavior was to be avoided at all cost. The irony is that it became an amusing lifetime chuckle, fondly told on JoAnn.

⚜

More than fitting, when telling of sharing life in the South Seas, it's mandatory to mention the opportunity to experience and soulfully appreciate the wonders offered by its unique ambiance, especially its exposition of beauty at the time of nearing darkness.

How many ways can one witness and absorb the fabulous gift of sunsets? Probably as many as actually occur, which is virtually daily. Everyone has their list of enthrall. When observed and absorbed from beaches and hidden coves, from rocky points, verandas, and upper floor balconies, while in flight, and, of course, from the decks of all sized boats when sailing all sorts of waters, they are never a disappointment. Each viewing is memorable and whether in a group or alone, they are always rich in inspiration and especially resplendent in romance.

A sight not often mentioned is the calculated monthly rising of the moon, especially when viewed from a schooner deck while floating on a lagoon. Its awesome impact is truly a treat worthy of a reverent thank you for the grant of the passing day and a toast to a safe and secure, sleep-full night and another appreciated tomorrow.

⋄

For some reason, the fall of tropical rain or even a sudden squall, while attending an outdoor movie was always a source of shared closeness. No one would question that it's the situation and circumstance that provides the beneficial accentuation to any event, whatever its intent.

I honestly feel that over our many, many mutually enriching years, JoAnn too always felt that each occasion we shared was positive, just and heaven sent.

RMH

5-2012

Her Wedding Shower, Kwajalein

Sailing on The Lagoon, Kwajalein, M.I.

Scuba, Anyone?, Kwajalein, M.I.

Diamond Head View, Honolulu, HI

New Years on Kwajalein, M.I.

Storm on Milford Sound, New Z.

Kwajalein On The Lagoon

A splendid addition to the unique and enviable lifestyle provided to the fortunate alumni of Kwajalein was its lagoon that extended its diversion opportunities far out onto the water. Beyond the facilities for organized activities, and beach offerings of sun bathing, reef snorkeling and wind surfing, were the adventures of scuba diving and the joy of sailing. The latter, for some, was an avocation.

When it came to the world of sailing, my inexperience was bolstered by a state of total non-awareness. My participation, much as that of Blanche DuBoise of "*Street Car*" fame, "relied upon the kindness of strangers". As fortune would have it, I had JoAnn. She was well attached to sailing friends, which, like so many of our Kwajalein ties, we maintained for decades. As grateful invited guests over many island years, we maintained an ample log of sailing indulgences, several remembered as adventures.

Kwajalein's sheltered lagoon offered a vast expanse of calm water, a reliable breeze, and a multitude of island inlets and beaches. A dedicated group of "yachting people" acquired and owned, lovingly maintained, and used a variety of sail boats, after which, they then gathered to enthusiastically share their inspired "sea" stories. Their devotion to this activity matched that of their on-land devotees of golf and tennis.

The only group that may have exceeded the yachtsmen in this regard, were the Vets Hall drinkers. Sailing and scuba diving were a major morale program.

Over time we enjoyed the opportunity to "check out" the hospitality offerings of virtually the entire fleet anchored at Kwajalein. Cal 20 sailboats were the staple. They were available for checkout by licensed sailors, with several more being privately owned after being acquired as used excess and then lovingly rehabbed. Added to these were another off and on half dozen 35' /42' / 55' to 60' yacht sized boats, which had been sailed down from Hawaii or California to round out the fleet. Don and Krista, a popular couple, had their boat built in Taiwan and bravely sailed it down from there. The Yacht Club members were a hearty, courageous and close-knit group. We owe much to Dick and Ann and Al and so many valiant others.

Whether weekly or occasionally, or if even only once, sailing on the lagoon offered the stimulating thump and spray of the waves, the invigorating freshness of the sea breezes, and pure fun of sail mate bonding, which was always accompanied by the ritual of beverages and a picnic. Often an occasional squall added to the thrill. All and all, as a way of life, it's hard to beat.

JoAnn was actively involved in sailing and, bless her, she even ventured into scuba diving. She passed on tennis and team sports, only dabbled at golf, but did demonstrate a strong interest in dining and dancing and party guesting. Also, as she progressed in living quarters, she became an eager hostess. Who ever had such an "accidental" life? The God of Good Fortune earned our enduring gratitude.

RMH

6-2016

The Spell Of Ponape

It was in the early, spirited phase of our relationship that the first spark stirred the senses of adventure and curiosity within JoAnn. She was enthusiastic throughout the planning and entire experience of our off-island venture to Ponape. It turned out to be life changing.

Only on a personal visit, with an attitude of open abandonment, could anyone truly begin to appreciate the ambience of Ponape. A descriptive narrative is inadequate to its primitive naturalness. I'll relate a few remembrances that were touching and memorable for us.

Ponape is a small island located in the Caroline Islands. We traveled there by air. After landing we journeyed through Kolonia, a ramshackle main village, past homes on stilts in the jungle with small domestic livestock lulling around below. The semi rough road led us a quarter way around the island to the hill sited, large, thatch roofed Village Hotel. Its principle feature was a spacious open veranda oriented for activities, dining and a spectacular view.

Guest accommodations were small huts similarly thatched with a similar view. They were scattered about along connected pathways that meandered back to their master lodge. The primary activity for us on this holiday was unfettered fun. The fact that we were well beyond our carefree and silly years, speaks to the infectious essence of Ponape.

We traversed trails throughout the hills and romped with native children who introduced us to secluded waterfalls and nature adorned swimming pools where we wildly soaked and splashed in revelry. We boated around the reefs to delve out the mystery of the huge stone structured, lost to the ages, canal designed city of Nan Modal.

During tropical rainfalls we remained snug and secure by entrenching on our open veranda where we refuged to play games, devour pupus and savor rum punch. We hiked nature paths and visited the village. A chuckle for me was watching JoAnn gleefully swinging while wedged in a makeshift seat at the end of a 30 foot rope tied to the top of a swaying, leaning palm.

I firmly believe that the extraordinary joy of our Ponape excursion directly influenced the thinking that formulated our future travel filled lifestyle. Having stuck our toes in to test the water, we found the delights of Ponape to be more than an adequate incentive for us to venture out even further into the world.

Ponape stimulated our anticipation, Kwajalein provided the opportunity; the rest became our remarkable history.

RMH

9-2011

Northern California

I picked up JoAnn near San Mateo at the airport that serves the city of San Francisco. With huge anticipation and bursting with enthusiasm and smugness, I immediately drove her to the Coit Tower Plaza to launch our first extended holiday with its impressive dramatic view of one of the world's great cities.

One wonderful aspect about JoAnn was her innocence and open-ness to grandeur and new experiences. And I was on my turf. I had worked and lived in San Francisco twice and in my teens had hung out there quite often.

This important first travel together experience was to be her intro-duction to Northern California. It was to begin with a presentation of San Francisco to a most deserving, seemingly sheltered, sweet Southern lady. JoAnn had already become the essence and purpose of my life, so, for me, this venture was a very big deal. The marvel of San Francisco is that it is more than adequate to serve as a dramatic and splendid be-ginning to any special journey.

The initial view from the Coit Tower veranda overlooks North Beach and Fisherman's Wharf. As your view sweeps left from the Bay Bridge out across the picturesque bay it passes Alcatraz and distant Sausilito and arrives to dwell upon the magnificent Golden Gate

Bridge. Your sight then lifts over Chinatown on up to Nob Hill. Somehow this rich panoramic feast is comforting in the gentleness of its at-home-feeling of welcome.

Though impressive as a city and stunning in setting, San Francisco has a sense of being small. Wherever you look or wander you are entertained with interesting sights, but you never feel overwhelmed. Maybe its hills lend isolating individuality to its assortment of renowned and infamous neighborhoods.

From the Buena Vista near the wharf, where I often breakfasted, one can take a cable car up the hill past the famous hotels and down Powell Street into Union Square. From there stroll Geary Street, view the city from the Top-of-the-Mark, and though no longer a wondrous little shop, check out the ever uniqueness of Gumps, and, for convenience pass through the inviting arched entry-way off Union Square for an absolute-must foray of Chinatown.

When driving around to challenge the hills and unique Lombard Street, one must not fail to visit everyman's back yard, the vast Golden Gate Park. Also drive all the way thru the Presidio area for an astounding upward view from the footing area below the fabulous Golden Gate Bridge.

And then drive on to the breathtaking treat of crossing this awesome and famous span to enjoy the view of it and its equally famous city from the vantage point of Sausilito.

Without mentioning sports venues and museums, or restaurants and delis offering seafood and pasta and pastry, know that San Francisco is a memorable destination all of its own.

We next moved on, departing the city on the ridge route that travels above Burlingame, Palo Alto and Santa Clara, and then at San Jose we caught the freeway on to Santa Cruz. Our next playground would be Monterey, Carmel and Big Sur. As all who know, this is a truly stunning, heaven-blessed area. It is the home of Pebble Beach, quaint seashore villages, impressive homes, and awesome geography that, weather permitting, offers fabulous views from roads, trails and beaches. It is spectacular, beautiful, charming and even quaint, all in one. I believe hiking in Big Sur is where JoAnn got the poison oak on her bottom.

We next crossed the state with visits to wineries in Salinas, and a bed and breakfast stopover in a small old west hotel in Merced. Our destination was Yosemite National Park. From the time of the two summers when as a teenager I camped on the ground with kids from all over the state, Yosemite Valley has marinated with other visits throughout my life into becoming my personal "cathedral". It is truly a reverent place. For me, it was a mandatory stop with JoAnn. I believe its splendor performed its special miracle, while also eradicating the poison oak.

We then wended our way through the old gold towns on up the Sierras to Lake Tahoe. This is a mountain lake paradise with ski lodges, cabins, a village with casinos, and roads that sweep down to Virginia City and Reno in Nevada and back up to circle the lake. And wouldn't you know, possibly just for JoAnn, the Gatlin Brothers and Roger Miller performed for us, along with a few hundred other guests, of course.

To complete the tour, we went north and then west over Donner Pass and then descended the mountains to venture through Sacramento, the state capital. From there, we veered over to the Bay to visit Vallejo, the hometown of my high school days. As such visits may appear to everyone, the school seemed to have shrunk and was nostalgically ancient and sadly faded.

With one more powerful panoramic look in store for her, a viewing of San Francisco from the Oakland side of the Bay while traversing the hugely impressive Bay Bridge, our introductory compatibility tour was concluded at the airport where I had so eagerly picked her up. JoAnn went on to Texas to visit with her family in San Antonio. I went back to Kwajalein where I started my vigil for her return to the island to relate her personal report on our excursion.

And, most of all, for her decision as to the status of my place in her life.

RMH

9-2011

Part II

Our Lifestyle

Compatibility

Opportunity

Adventures

Trips & Treks

Like others, there were earlier years when I had work related occasions that included travel, which, due to my possession of a curiosity bent, were not only interesting but stimulating, exciting, and life formulating. For me, they were mostly trips from Los Angeles to New York City.

To be sure, leisure travel is much more fun. On business trips, personal interests are secondary and often very limited in terms of being a travel experience. When working, your concentration and most of your waking time is job oriented. Any focus allotted to curiosity or personal fun must generally be stolen from your off the job or sleeping hours, so the effort can become a bit stressful. Pleasure travel is more "footloose and fancy free".

JoAnn and I were lucky in that most of our travel experience would be described as leisure. Any stress was just part of the thrill. Of course we had to foot the bill, so to speak, but that too worked out fortuitously. Along with the 'means' and both of us being endowed with 'curiosity', the number one essential for the undertaking of adventure travel, our unique situation further granted us the third necessity for travel, 'time'. Possessing a reasonable amount of stamina, good health, and a perfect, compatible companion to share the experience with also rank high as favorable recommendations.

Happily that's the way it was for us.

JoAnn's worldly excursions began with visits to exotic cities and regions on the east coast of Asia with alternating tours throughout several nations of southern Europe and the Mediterranean. These trips were launched from, and after, her journey to the far-reaching location of Kwajalein Island in the Marshall Islands in the South Pacific. They continued over a period of ten years.

Treks to desired destinations in the whole of North America and the Caribbean followed after relocation back to Huntsville, Alabama. All in all, the opportunity of travel adventure greatly invigorated and enriched her life. My belief is that she found all of it to be immensely satisfying.

As an on scene voyeur to virtually all of her excursions, I am pleased to attest as to how each of her lovable traits of enthusiasm, excitement, and wonder responded to each event. It was a blessing to see and share it all as an official, first hand witness to her eager, bold and fearless plunge into her first viewing of some of the world's wonders. It was pure joy for me; think what a life altering experience it was for her.

Suffice it to say, as paraphrased in song to the heroine of Camelot, "never would I have missed seeing you in such moments of enthusiasm, awe, and thrill."

RMH
3-2016

Testament To: Her Enthusiasm

Happily I can attest to the exhilaration generated by JoAnn's *eagerness and enthusiasm* as we shared the planning and packing for our month long, annual treks.

It perpetuated on to every boarding of planes, ships and trains, buses, barges, rental cars, and ferry and excursion boats. Going and doing were important to JoAnn. Once there, she embraced gondolas on the canals of Venice, jet boats on the shallow rivers of New Zealand, and a row boat in and out the Blue Grotto of Capri.

Another batch of conveyances she eagerly boarded were cable cars and trams. Destination sites included: Victoria Peak for hiking views of Hong Kong, Kowloon and Aberdeen and for dinners, up the "other" acropolis hill in Athens, and a special overview of Queenstown, New Zealand; a unique, panorama view of Singapore while crossing over to its park on Sentosa Island; and for breath-taking rides up Rigi near Lucerne and Zugspitze near Garmisch. I believe a funicular took us up the giant hill overlooking Ching Mai. I know we descended by foot down the long, "dragon-bannistered" staircase. Thailand as an adventure was exceptionally exotic for JoAnn.

Elevators served as conveyances in assorted towers such as the Eiffel in Paris and its cousin in Tokyo. They served the same purpose in other elevated view restaurants in New York, Seattle and Montreal.

A helicopter took us for a close up view of Mt. Cook and a landing on its glacier, where a snow ball fight added playful zest to our memorable excursion on New Zealand's South Island.

Our several stopovers in Hong Kong actually found us housed in convenient hotels in Kowloon. For us, Hong Kong was a remarkable view by day and an especially stunning sight at night. JoAnn and I made all of our assaults on Hong Kong by way of an always thrilling ride on the "Star Ferry".

JoAnn's enthusiasm carried on unabated when it came to prowling, romping, or simply strolling the streets, paths, and trails of a remarkable array of major and minor cities, towns, and villages, as well as exploring palace grounds, factory areas, markets, parks and arboretums. Not to be left out were such places as the glow worm caves above Milford Sound, the salt mines of Berchtesgaden, and the Shinto Shrines and Deer Park in Japan, the Taroka Gorge and marble quarry on Taiwan, and our sampling of the tapas bars of Madrid and Seville. She was unstoppable. She also possessed a yen for shopping.

Perhaps due to the past popularity of *"The Sound of Music"*, JoAnn really took to Salzburg when we stopped there on our earlier grand tour. Whatever, it's aura of ambience, spirit and flavor made a strong enough impression on JoAnn for us to re-route the plan for our Bavarian visit; we reversed the circle of our route from Munich so as to begin in Salzburg. When you visit, or if you have, you will fully understand and appreciate the wholesome and good senses possessed by JoAnn.

One aspect of JoAnn's behavior that extolled the kindness of her nature was her attraction to animals. For some reason she was drawn to the act of patting the noses of the police horses we encountered in London, Seville and New York and likewise with carriage horses when we rode in the parks. She was downright enthusiastic over her short rides on an elephant in Thailand and a camel in Egypt. Perhaps I shouldn't relate how she girlishly climbed aboard the back of a lion statue at a park in Delphi, Greece. Such was the spontaneity of JoAnn. It was beyond touching to behold the joy in her heart.

RMH
2-2015

Testament To: Her Astonishment

Happily I can attest to JoAnn's *awe and astonishment* when she encountered unexpected phenomenon of nature or extraordinary structures of mankind while traveling. This randomly ordered short list are candidates recommended as being worthy of personal review:

Meteora, located in Kalabaka, deep in the mountains of Greece, is a land formation that is overwhelmingly awesome when come upon unexpectedly. JoAnn and I gaped in disbelief as we climbed about. The formation was populated and functional; I recall that JoAnn was asked to purchase and don a more proper full-length skirt for entry into the religious sanctuaries.

Though renowned as a photographic classic, Neuschwanstein Castle was still a stunning standout among the sites visited on our expansive Bavarian holiday. We had mapped out an extensive visit which included all of King Ludwig's "monumental" domiciles. The trip was fabulous; JoAnn related to Germany and I related to the beer.

St. Peter's Cathedral, Sistine Chapel and Vatican Museum and a papal blessing dedication by the Pope to all the visitors congregated in the courtyard that Sunday were meaningful and far beyond expectation. Our entire tour of Italy provided us with a rich store of memories.

The importance of Buddha in the Orient is not hidden if for no other reason than the broad display of the impressive size and powerful images of <u>Buddhist statuary</u> on view from Japan to Thailand. The great Diabutsu and Reclining Buddha are highlights. The devotion to them is equally impressive.

Among the Greek Islands, <u>Santorini</u> is a stellar star. One's impression may not be adequately stirred until after they land and ascend up the trail to the city on top. JoAnn was in ecstasy riding her mule and then romping the byways throughout this majestic, blue-accented white city. Her viewing of Santorini was savored with unexpected awe and blessed with abandoned joy and perfect weather.

Family reasons placed us in Bangkok twice, and we strolled the <u>Imperial Palace</u> on both occasions for understandable reason. For a dramatic artistic statement that says "Far East", one must consider the exotic architecture and lore of Thailand (Siam). We had a thorough taste of its many flavors.

If seeking a quiet surprise, find yourself leaving the southwest area of Lake Constance and the German/Swiss city of the same name. Before hopping on the ferry back up into Germany, first find the bridge-way onto the tiny island of <u>Mainau</u>. Just as JoAnn and myself, you will never regret it.

<u>Ronda</u>, Spain is not a colorful or quaint village, but it is situated and structured upon one of the most awesome sites one could ever see or imagine. From our hotel room balcony we could toast the world as we looked out at seven layers of mountains, and down, where the birds flew beneath us, to view the miniature farms and animals far below. Salute another awesome wonder when venturing with JoAnn.

I'm unsure as to what this says about JoAnn, but under awe and astonishing it seems proper to mention two sites: The <u>Topkapi Palace</u> in Istanbul, Turkey and the <u>Tower</u> of London. The reason is to lend descriptive definition for JoAnn's reaction to her review of their displays of "crown jewels".

RMH

3-2015

Blue Grotto, Capri, Italy

Toledo, on a touring visit of Spain

Santorini Island, Greece

Kamakura Daibutsu Buddha, Japan

Blue Mosque, Istanbul, Turkey

Sea or Lake Harbor, So. Europe

Change of Guard, London, England

Obergammergau, Bavaria

Great Pyramid, Giza, Egypt

Dragon Stairs, Ching Mai, Thailand

Fifth Stop-Over in Hong Kong, China

Seville, on a Tour of Spain

Neuschwanstein Castle, Bavaria

St. Moritz, Switzerland

Testament To: Her Excitement

Happily I can attest to JoAnn's *thrill and excitement* when first standing face to face with iconic travel symbols as they posed, majestically positioned, in their renowned surroundings. This is a selection of a few of such, "I never dreamed I'd ever see", highlight sights that she was granted the good fortunate to have visited while traveling. At their moment they elicited enthrall and would thereafter become a few of her favorite personal memories.

If for no other reason than its status on this wish list of most travelers, it begins with the Eiffel Tower in Paris, France. We took pictures of it, walked around it, climbed in it, and ate within it. Its dominance within the city is magnetic. However, much of the awe of it all must be ceded to Paris and its stunning self: Its incomparable ambiance; its streets, avenues, boulevards and buildings; its Louvre, Notre Dame Cathedral, Arc de Triomphe, and Sacre Coeur; its Sienne River walkways and bridges; and its shops, eateries, people, and nightlife. All are a stunning keepsake at the top of her bucket list.

I won't try to ascertain why JoAnn became so alive with excitement when we arrived and began our immersion in Italy's canal/island city of Venice. It could have been from having read romance novels. The city's mystical, imaginative look and incomprehensible watery setting boggles the mind. Our motor launch arrival up the Grand Canal and boating tour of Murano and Burano islands added to the event, to be sure. The wistful exploration of its many nooks, canals and activities made an indelible mark on JoAnn. Our stay was memorable; for her the visit was fabulous!

We had stopped in <u>New York</u> a couple of times, but it was on our first real visit that I witnessed the anticipation JoAnn expressed for going out to the <u>Statue of Liberty</u>. This holiday tour was truly eventful for her. She was full of eager zest as we hit most of my old haunts and stalked the whole of Manhattan. We also added to our booking list of shows. She was so enamored and smitten with NYC that she later braved a "solo" buddy visit with her daughter, Donna. I was never more proud of her for this display of spunk!

It was not Big Ben or Westminster Abbey, but the royal pageantry of "the changing of the guard" at <u>Buckingham Palace</u> that impressed JoAnn the most about <u>London</u> - that and the Tower and its maze of streets, pubs, activity, and theatrical shows. It was all a huge entertainment just for us. As a plus, it began and concluded our lengthy first tour of Europe.

With time available after our cruise of the Greek Islands, our visit to <u>Egypt</u> was not an after thought. Being feasible, it was planned as an exotic "bonus". Cairo with the <u>Pyramids</u> and Sphinx, and Luxor with its incredible <u>Karnak,</u> and the Valley of Kings and Queens left us in awe with their irrepressible impression. The unimaginable unique became astonishing, real and remarkable. Our papyrus print of the *"Wedding Couple"* is a happy keepsake.

Our extensive driving tour throughout south <u>New Zealand</u> can only be recorded as an enjoyable blast. JoAnn especially praised the food, but I best remember her exaltation when a ferocious storm suddenly struck us as we cruised <u>Milford Sound</u> and 1,000 waterfalls began to spout out of the walled cliffs. This trip was truly an adventure for her memory bank.

RMH

4-2015

Testament To: Her Comfort Zone

My testaments of JoAnn's responses to her many travel stimulants are personal and therefore subject to having been tweaked relevant to the importance of each subject and moment. That said, I am happy to attest to what I know to be her true temperament. JoAnn was always open, friendly and secure when feeling unpretentious and independent. She preferred being *comfortable, coddled and cozy.*

JoAnn was most mellow in small towns and villages, or in small spaces in large towns or great cities. This is probably why, after our long, very successful comprehensive tour, we thereafter traveled on our own, utilizing local tours, or taxi drivers when in ports on cruises to take in the local sights. Which is also why our trips are long-listed with surprising discoveries populated with unexpected sights, food, and people. If you get the chance, drop in on Bodrum, Delphi, Granada, Innsbruck, Lindau, Mejas, Toledo, or, St. Moritz, and Rothenburg ob der Tauber or any town in So. New Zealand. It's worth the effort to seek out the nooks of Madrid or Munich, Venice or Vienna, or crannies of Athens, Bangkok, Cairo, Istanbul, Kyoto, Singapore, or Taipai. JoAnn's store of stamina was far above normal.

Our search for comfort, cozy and fun spots included the usual, such as Raffles in Singapore, Haufbrau House in Munich, Ned Kelly's in

Kowloon and Mona Vale in Christchurch. Some unexpected treats were great hamburgers at Wolfe's in London, picnics overlooking white villages in Spain, luaus on beaches in the Fiji Islands, and having breakfast in Dunedin accompanied by a jazz trio.

Not to be overlooked as entertainment are the rituals of Hula, Kabuki, Thai, Can Can, Flamenco, Greek men, and Turkish men and ladies performing sword/fire and belly dances. We much preferred the garden and park concerts, and the never before seen light and water shows of Karnak, Egypt and Sentosa Island, Singapore.

JoAnn was very partial to religious shrines and cathedrals, and whether in the Far East or Europe they were in abundance. No matter their size or impression of magnificence or might, they were always places of tranquility and sanctuary. All religions are expressive and unique in their architecture which is obviously important and culturally very interesting. One of note, discovered by JoAnn in a guidebook, is the Ottobeuren Basilika in Bavaria. If ever nearby, don't miss it.

The activity of shopping is not remotely exclusive to JoAnn, yet it cannot be overlooked for comment. Rather than dwelling on her pursuits of jewelry in such places as Toba, Japan, the home of Mikimota pearls, and Bangkok for serious viewing, Hong Kong for creative effort, Amsterdam for diamond study, and a shop in Singapore that mailed Christmas cards to her for 20 years, I'll address her unique efforts that mostly concerned her family. She labored at this with genuine, over-the-top, loving care.

Keep in mind, this was important to JoAnn. Some items were shipped directly, others were "lugged" home to be mailed or personally delivered. Randomly recalled were leather handbags from Kusadasi, Turkey, papyrus prints from Cairo, carved netsukes from Hong Kong, beer steins from Memmingen, Bavaria, and the infamous sheepskin rugs from New Zealand. Some personal collectables were a silk prayer rug from Istanbul, a wood carving from Oberammergau, artwork from Granada, Rothenburg, Taipei and Cairo, liqueur bottles from Vienna and Sorrento, lace from Burano, and silk pillows and custom made clothes from Bangkok. Remarkably, these efforts were accomplished in our spare time.

For a brief span of time, JoAnn may not have ever ruled the world, but she made the most of the little spaces she occupied at her special moments. I can attest to that.

RMH
5-2015

Show Time

Possibly the one thing I can claim to have introduced to JoAnn was the theater. She took to musical theater ravishingly - plays and symphony, not so much. Overseas on our travels, the only theater that we really took to was in London. It was so successful that JoAnn started a collection of theater jackets. Another thing the experience confirmed to me is that our fate or luck regarding attendance was fully under the control of her personal karma.

Our first journey to Europe departed from Hawaii, which necessitated a full day of air travel. We arrived in London in the morning, still drowsy, took a nap and shower, found out where we were, jumped on the subway to rush downtown, and started hiking. This was our pace for 20 years.

Not too far along, somewhere not much beyond Covent Garden, we came upon a theater with a long line out front. I hopped ahead into the lobby and made inquiries and came out with two tickets to *Cats*. The theater was in the round and the performance was a smash hit. The next night, again we saw a sold out show featuring England's renowned Rowan Atkinson. It was a laugh hit with a lifetime's worth of British humor. During the daytime we toured the amazing sights of London.

On the fourth day we were prowling and came upon the Palladium Theater. Again I went inside and inquired after tickets and lo, I acquired two cancellations. To avoid the hassle, we decided to stay downtown and, after high tea, more browsing, and then an early dinner, we strolled over to the theater.

The street fronting the theater was closed - Kleig lights were beaming into the sky and limos were disgorging richly attired, gorgeous people. The scene was teeming with humanity; every theater person in London was in attendance. It was the opening night of "La Cage et Foles". Our seats were in orchestra and we were dressed in our grubbies. The man next to me said his friends had tried to get tickets for over three months. No, I did not break the heart of the man's friend; after all, it was merely another karma-produced evening at the theater for JoAnn.

Some three weeks later, having completed our introductory tour of Europe, we were back in London. Once again we arrived in the morning, and again, a bit drowsy from a huge evening at a farewell party in Brussels. As before, we rested up and then mosied out to a late lunch or early dinner after which we wandered around a bit and stumbled upon another all lit-up, teeming with people, musical theater where karma promptly placed us in two choice seats. The show was a revival of "42nd Street".

The next day was our last in London. Our holiday was over and our long return home was ahead. We slept in, had a leisurely lunch and decided to visit the British Museum. Strolling back through SoHo, again we found ourselves before a grand theater, which this time presented us with a major dilemma. The musical showing was the recently opened, soon to be hugely successful, "Les Miserables". Once again I entered the lobby and once again JoAnn's karma performed its magic; our two tickets were available for that nights performance.

The show was ours to see. However, we paused to question our-selves - should we be excited over our good luck or, were we "theatered" out? Did we want to be by ourselves? I don't remember the full con-versation, but I recall that we had a cozy, candlelit Italian dinner, which was followed with a private toast to our fabulous holiday with cham-pagne and strawberries in our room.

RMH

4-2014

For Goodness Sake

Some things require the force of nature, a powerful thrust of motivation, an exceptional reason, or the application of all three in a cohesive plan of action that will mount an effort sufficient enough to assure a successful outcome to a very personal, special purpose.

Our cause did the trick. It was loaded with good intentions for all concerned!

What possible reason or force could motivate Mr. and Mrs. Curtis Pennington, JoAnn's father and step- mother from San Antonio, Texas, JoAnn's two sons, Greg and Doug and their families with three grandchildren, to fly, most for the very fist time, to rendezvous at her daughter, Donna and husband Larry's home in Longwood, Florida, just North of Orlando, for a rare family reunion?

Of course, as a purpose, this act of togetherness all by itself was worthy enough, but there was more. JoAnn added close friends; Ann and Betty drove down from Alabama. Boots and other friends, discovered to be traveling in Florida, were contacted and diverted to the activity and, as it sometimes happens, by chance while out shopping, other island friends were encountered on the streets of Winter Park who were instantly added to the event. The occasion also demanded a personal jaunt of over 6,000 miles. What would cause such a frenzy of effort?

Such an inquiry is perfectly reasonable only if asked by someone totally unfamiliar with the situation.

The long-planned, logistically-challenging, very important occasion, was JoAnn's wedding to Ray.

For JoAnn's family, the episode had its mysteries to be sure, and its curiosities for certain. Historically, a primary daughter and much-loved mother came out of the cold, and a grand family bonding came off as a joyous, happy occasion. It was splendid and special for all. The adults experienced a Florida holiday, and the children and adults shared a Disney World adventure. It was a festive, positive celebration, chock full of lasting, good memories for all.

It also witnessed two grown-up, somewhat untethered individuals happily reach out to consummate new family ties in an important, ceremonious manner. We never discussed it out loud, but if we had, we may have smugly said, "If undeserving of this expansion of our newly found 'being-together' happiness in any way, we choose not to question it. Thank you very much."

With this portion of our annual excursion complete, as a now fully committed we, our next leg was to board a plane out of Orlando for our flight to Athens, Greece. We had booked a stay in a very stately, regal hotel from which we toured all the city sites and historic ruins, and arranged for venture tours over to Delphi and down to Olympia on Peloponese, and up to the historical legendary war areas, and further on up into the mountains to Kalabaka for an unforgettable viewing of awesome Meteora.

After touring the historic sites of Greece, we then boarded the Stella Maris, a cozy Italian cruise ship booked for JoAnn's especially planned honeymoon cruise of the Greek Islands.

Our small ship was character saturated with a rich assortment of wealthy passengers. There were couples, groups and families from

South America, Australia, and Canada, and even Texas. The entire cruise was casual, hugely impressive, and full of fun. The Australians brought their 'needles', the Texan doctor went out of his way to take our souvenir pictures, and Doctor John and Cindy, our Canadian table mates, ended up exchanging Christmas letters with us for the next twenty years. And, as always, the Latinos entertained everyone with their devotion to dance.

The enthusiasm was contagious as we made our assaults of the stunning, renowned islands of Mykonos and Santorini, and the remarkable historic islands of Crete and Rhodes, and fun frolics on several other unique, smaller islands. Our cruise tour included fabulous adventure stopovers at Istanbul, Kusidasi, Ephisis and Bodrum in Turkey. While in the region, we extended our tour with an astonishing visit to Cairo and Giza, and Luxor and Karnak in Egypt.

Our honeymoon holiday was beyond memorable. The cruise was our first, and the impression it made on JoAnn, inculcated her with its carefree, luxurious way of life in a manner that kept the opportunity for booking cruises at the top of our excursion list for the rest of our fairy tale lives.

RMH
12-2016

FOOD, Drink & Travel

As an alternative to gossip and innuendo, polite social exchange turns to food, drink and travel. Such conversation is generally embraced with eager and enthusiastic participation. Food and dining are way beyond being simple endeavors, they are an essential for life, and the essence of lifestyle.

The revelry of a fun evening with enjoyable friends over a lengthy fondue dinner inspired the writing of this narrative. Actually, it was probably the humorous nature of our conversation that spawned the topic. Buried admidst the amusing repartee was a friendly ribbing over the grave innocence of my never before having participated in the so-phisticated novelty of the fondue experience. Though neglectfully sad, this error had now been happily remedied and it turned the evening into a celebration of my accomplishment.

The recall of this occasion forms the gist of these dining experiences. This is not a discussion about food preparation or recipes. I lack even a minor apprentice credential when it comes to wondrous dishes or proper diet. These anecdotes, much as the lively conversation at our fondue evening, tell of a few favored remembrances and amusing incidents involving dining mishaps and joys that were shared on travels with JoAnn.

To be sure, each of these occasions deserve an elaborate build-up to give them the importance that they merit considering the value of their punch lines. At least, to me. Instead, I'll rely upon your imagination to elaborate on their place and settings, and to fill the necessary decorative elements that emphasize their anecdotal worth.

❦

I'll begin with some calamities. The top story must, of course, have happened in Paris. For enchantment and romance, it's hard to beat the flavor of a foreign city, a beautiful evening, and a special table at an open-air restaurant on the Avenue Des Champs Elysees amidst the nightlife of Paris.

I remember that we actually enjoyed our struggle with the menu. We didn't ask for assistance and none was offered. The beverages and early courses went smoothly. The entrees arrived with fanfare. My order was presented beautifully and the aroma of JoAnn's selection was rapturous. The anticipation for the first taste was exhilarating. JoAnn raised her fork and knife and eagerly commenced to slice. She easily went through the soft gristle to the bone. We had ordered a "hoof" - so much for sophistication. The waiter was called. I apologized, and he was gallant. He didn't even smirk as he assisted us in a satisfying reorder, all in admirable English.

❦

The estrangement everyone sensed when first visiting an especially different land, amplifies everything you see, hear and taste. We were at a high pitch all the while we were in the city of Taipei on Taiwan.

As background, Joann and I lived and worked with a variety of technical type engineers and their assortment of wives on a small American compound in the Marshall Islands. In all, it was a very worldly community. We were acquainted with Tommy, the wife of a computer technician. She was Chinese and her native home had been Taipei. When we stopped in Taiwan on our planned, once-a-year monthly holiday, this time to the Orient, much to our surprise and good fortune, there was Tommy.

Probably, through the osmosis of our close island lifestyle, Tommy had learned of our visit and, being on home leave, she had voluntarily assigned herself as our hospitality hostess and guide. Her brother, as it happened, was a major executive with the Taiwanese Airline. He loaned his sister the use of his Mercedes and the driver services of his son, Tommy's nephew. Needless to say, our visit went quite well.

An exceptional treat for us was an honorary gesture the family bestowed upon Tommy. A family dinner was arranged for her American guests at a sumptuous Chinese hotel. Not at the Madame Chiang Kai-Shek spectacular, lacquer red Grand Hotel, but it was held in a private room.

The entire family was seated at place settings around a large round table. Gratefully, there was much chatter and ado among all of the old and young adults, men and women, and several children. No one spoke English. I say grateful, because in a room of silence, our nervous awkwardness would not have allowed us to survive the intensity of all the staring and scrutiny.

The food arrived and kept on arriving. It was placed in the center of the table, which was then spun slowly around to provide access to all. It seemed that the dictate of proper politeness was for everyone to partake and sample each dish, which we did. We experienced a great quantity and extensive variety of Chinese dishes. I, for one, did not recognize even one morsel of food.

The honor and ceremony of the affair was honestly appreciated, but the nervous aspect of being an object of curiosity, and the strain of controlling an inner gastric revolt, made the occasion more of a re-membered event, than a remarkable feast.

There were two things that I do recall. One was that chicken feet are a high delicacy and they were to be served only to Mama San, Tommy's mother. The other was, when we were well along in the meal and I was down to just nibbling, I learned that a sea cucumber was not a nutritional veggie, but a chewy "slug" that crawls on the bottom of the sea.

⁂

Madrid, Spain is a large city, but not huge. It has attractive buildings and grand boulevards with many dramatic turn-about circles that sur-round impressive, statue accented fountains. In the daytime it is stim-ulating to stroll about. At night, it's different.

The streets that throng with people are smaller, with many seeming to be more like alleys. This is where you find the tapas bars and clubs, and thriving restaurants. There are grander places, of course, including the popular area around the Plaza Mayor.

We liked the throngs, even when I was humiliated. It happened in a small, packed restaurant. On our way to our table, as we squeezed in, I noticed an appealing dish being served to a guy at the bar. We were settled and far into our meal with all going enjoyably well, surrounded by equally joyous patrons, when I got the idea to try the dish I saw on the way in.

Now, to be clear, except between JoAnn and I, nothing was con-ducted in English. Everything was accomplished with a lot of smiling. I motioned to the waiter, and even got up to point out the delicacy I saw, and requested an order.

The revelry went on. Shortly the dish arrived. I served some to JoAnn and myself, and then took a sizeable fork full, hoping for a culinary delight. Shockingly to my taste, it was awful. Equally stunning, I learned that it was brains.

When I told the waiter to take it away, all in gestures, he was not pleased. However, all of our surrounding pleasant patron friends roared with laughter. The bumbling matador had been duly gored.

❧

On the more joyous and fond memory side of the food ledger, when it comes to good tasting, easy to order, comfort food, JoAnn would give the nod to New Zealand. She'd get no quarrel from me. Another unique phenomenon that comes to mind is the only restaurant in our travels that we ever frequented three times. It was a converted house with a large patio in the old town section of San Diego. It served Mexican food. Perhaps we returned because of the fountain pool and the strolling mariachi band; that, and the fact that JoAnn was from San Antonio and loved Mexican food. I can't even recall how we ever got to San Diego three times.

❧

From a multitude of pleasant dining experiences, the first that comes to mind is an evening on a veranda in Piazza Navona in the heart of Rome. The setting was recommended by Bob, our British tour guide. Because he knew every nook and cranny of Europe, our tour was fabulous, as was his selection of dining experiences. The piazza courtyard is renowned for its fountains and statuary. We ate by candlelight. The waiters were gracious. The menu was perfect. JoAnn was pleased, and I was a hero.

❧

If one travels and wishes to feel that they were a part of the world scene and its people, a communal dinner in Munich deserves consideration. The heart of old town is Marienplatz. It is a striking plaza from which several streets off shoot to other interesting places. On one street, one block over and around the corner, about the third door up toward the grand cathedral, is a small restaurant. When we entered, we found it well occupied with humanity and friendly banter. Whenever and wherever space is available, everyone is seated at one of the six-or-eight person tables.

We were directed to join two German gentlemen. We were greeted cheerfully. We looked at menus, but as usual, I looked around at others' dishes and pointed. We were well settled, when I glanced up and saw a couple enter the restaurant. I knew I recognized him, but not the lady. I consulted with JoAnn and she agreed. I stood up and waved them over to our table. The man was English and we had met him the evening before at the Haufbrau House. We now had a full table and surprise, surprise, everyone spoke English. Except for one of the German men who was a cousin visiting from East Germany. The wall had fallen a few months before.

It was a grand evening. The Germans talked excitedly about their business plans; the Englishman about his business on the continent, and his German girl friend about the seriousness of a considered marriage and where they might live. We talked and talked, and ate and ate, and drank a bit, too. It was a memorable dinner.

❧

Tokyo is huge. Not only that, but most people do not speak English, and all of the street signs, and billboards are in Chinese hieroglyphics, with menus occasionally assisted with plastic food replicas. To get around you learn very fast to follow the color codes. We got around by making use of buses, subways, taxis and even a barge. We strolled around numerous areas and ate in a variety of large and small restaurants.

One such lunch stop became one of the most touching experiences we had in all or our travels. The restaurant, with chrome and formica furnishings was somewhat like our old time drug stores, only much larger. As everywhere, it was packed full of life. We were finishing our lunch, when a young girl approached our table and politely addressed us in English. She spoke sweetly, and then asked permission for her father to come to our table to converse with us for the purpose of practicing his English. He was a school teacher. We were delighted, of course. We stammered through several topics, and then, in gratitude, he tried to instruct us in the essential expressions of politeness in Japanese. He used napkins, which I have in our scrapbook to this day. This occasion was truly one of our highest-of-quality lunch stops.

It's interesting how our favorite dining events are best remembered, not for the food, but as wondrous, life enriching memories.

RMH
3 -2012

Part III

Our Homeland

Families

Expansion

Appreciation

Aloha

To be fair to myself, our situation required that anyone wishing to exercise the annual leave clause in their employment contract it was necessary to pass through Hawaii. Twice. In a few years this would add up and could obviously alter one's viewpoint on the idea of visiting Hawaii, wouldn't it? Anyway that's the excuse I'm stuck with for the feeling of remorse I carry around within me for making my rude response to JoAnn's sweet cousin when she once politely asked me if Hawaii was "interesting".

JoAnn and I had enjoyed numerous stop-overs and a half dozen holiday visits which included four of the Hawaiian Islands, and yet, for some absurd reason, in comparing these wonderful holidays with our other more "worldly" excursions, my awkward response to the word "interesting" was shameful and totally inadequate. My weak answer was something like a dream busting, "It's ok".

Hawaii is a marvelous place to visit. But, as most islands, not for being interesting, but for their exotic ambiance and sense of release and abandonment from life's normal responsibilities. My response to JoAnn's cousin was too brief and far short of what was required for polite conversation, and I herein apologize to Connie, a wonderful, adorable lady.

A mere moment of reflection on JoAnn's experience concerning Hawaiian visits would have amply answered Connie's query. Her stopovers numbered in the dozens. JoAnn was comfortably familiar with the shops, eateries and beaches of Honolulu, and virtually all of the highlights of Honolulu, Oahu. We had toured the entire countenance of this renowned, bustling island, touching its highlights of Diamond Head, fluted cliffs of Kaneohe, surfing beaches, North Shore Resorts, renowned hotels and restaurants, and historic military facilities and sites. We had rejoiced at shows that featured Hawaiian culture and personalities, and had luckily attended parades and special events, and met special people.

Good fortune allowed us the opportunity to enjoy holiday visits to 3 more of these astonishing islands. An assortment of Hawaiian holidays are available with scheduled commute flights to each island. On all of our visits, we rented cars to fully experience the unique excursions they offered:

Kauai: the "Canyon" island offered rugged terrain, secluded resorts, a black sand beach and a golfing residence community on the windy plateau side.

Maui: the popular "Lush" island is more populated with grand resorts, wildlife sanctuaries, a high tech installation on a high-rise mountain, and unusual coastal drive to Hana.

Hawaii (The Big Island): the "Volcano" island is huge in size and awesome as an active, lava flowing reality. It features an historic area, a golf resort, ranches, farms and two villages, Hilo and Kona.

For JoAnn, all of this was augmented by special visits that included separate, treasured sight-seeing tours with her father and stepmother, and her daughter, Donna. Certainly, my apology is warranted.

However, this recollection of my debacle, conjured up the response our Asian travel agent made when I asked him about routing us down to Bali. He said, "You live on island, why you want go there?" We never went to Bali.

RMH
2-2014

The Other South

It was a few years down the road before I broached the idea of visiting Southern California. JoAnn and I had shared a couple of journeys by then. Our first being to the Far East for a tour of Tokyo and a selection of Japan's splendors, plus a first visit to Hong Kong. As best as I recall, this was also after our lengthy first tour of Europe. By then we had pretty well worked out the kinks in our annual month-off-the-island schedule.

I was somewhat eager to show her my "territory", and yet, for reasons I couldn't define I was also apprehensive. Most of the thirty years of my life before Kwajalein were centered in the Los Angeles area and my sense was that she might find it strange, or worse, feel uncomfortable.

Having covered the entire region extensively through every phase of my growing up life, I knew the area well. This even sort of included that of a child and teenager, which I had experienced through our son who was born in Hollywood and grew up in Pasadena. My school, family, play and working years took me into every hill and dale and beach of Southern California. This all began when there were still acres of orange groves, and long before there were hundreds of miles of freeways. It turned out my concern over JoAnn's reaction was totally unfounded.

Much different than the North, the Southern area of California is really more of a "way of life" than a place with a lot of remarkable things to see. The challenge of trying to show someone Los Angeles is that it's just a huge city and its primary feature is its ambiance – it's just there. The literally hundreds of towns of which it is comprised are all situated and blended upon a huge chunk of geography that flows down from a mountain backdrop, and then spreads across a valley desert that surrounds several prominent hills and merges with a vast alluvial flood plain that spreads down to miles and miles of sea shore. The shore is accented with an assortment of stunning beaches along a coastline that begins north of Santa Barbara and traverses all the way down to San Diego and the border at Baja California, Mexico.

The surprising thing about Southern California to most visitors is probably the mountains, which are fairly large and forested. They offer an opportunity for an abrupt change in lifestyle. The clusters of assorted hills add variety and interest to the terrain of the entire area. The next unexpected shock would be the vast amount of severe desert that covers all of the landscape on the East side of the mountains all the way to the Nevada and Arizona borders.

On this excursion, for some reason I had gone to the mainland ahead of JoAnn and had found a unique chalet lodge styled motel situated at the cross point of Wilshire Blvd. and what in the past was the old San Fernando Road that came up and over from the Valley. It had been long ago developed into the San Diego Freeway.

The freeway drops into the city near Westwood between Beverly Hills and Santa Monica and then proceeds on past the L.A. Airport and Long Beach, through Orange County, and on down to San Diego. This chalet lodge was our headquarters for the Los Angeles phase of JoAnn's exposition tour and, though it no longer exists, it served us well.

Rather than describe an itinerary of our wanderings, or give a simple list of specific highlights, for reasons stated, it may leave a better sense and feel of what Southern California has to offer by relating a variety of exposures JoAnn experienced as we took in the sights of the region.

For instance, from our chalet location it was easy to take Wilshire south to the Venice Beach and Santa Monica boardwalks and infamous "muscle beach" area, and then drive on the renowned PCH (Pacific Coast Highway) out to Malibu to have brunch at the Chart House for champagne with our lox and cream cheese on bagels and smoked salmon omelets. Next was a stop off at the original Getty Museum near Sunset Blvd., which we then took to drive inland to see the impressive area of Pacific Palisades, Brentwood, Bel Air, and Beverly Hills. After viewing some of the area's fine homes and famous pink Beverly Hills Hotel, while in the area, we visited my alma mater in Westwood, and as a must for JoAnn, we strolled the shops on Rodeo Drive.

Another drive on Sunset took us further up hill for a viewing of the LA basin from the famous "strip", and then on to Hollywood to take in Grauman's and Kodak Academy Award Theaters, the famous outdoor Bowl, and on over the hill to Universal City and the NBC studio for the Tonight Show with Jay Leno. Next on to Forest Lawn, the L.A. Zoo, and then across back over the hill to the Greek Theater, the Griffith Observatory for its overview of downtown, and then, to give JoAnn an exclusive bird's eye look, we took a meandering drive up the hill to the historic Hollywood (real estate) Sign.

For spectator entertainment there's the Walk of the Stars, farmer's market, restaurants of reputation, the spectacular development of downtown Los Angeles, the Doroth Chandler and Disney Theaters, and the taking in of horse racing at Hollywood Park where she spotted 3 movie/tv actors. We also visited Dodger Stadium for baseball when Pete Rose was the opposing team's manager and the Rose Bowl in Pasadena where later she would enjoy a college game when John Elway played for Stanford. Later on, with Ray's family she would be enthralled by attending the incomparable Rose Parade.

On day six we left our chalet headquarters and headed southward. After passing the airport and the beach oriented towns, we detoured to take in the ocean view from the cliffs of Palos Verdes Peninsula as we circled around and then down to the L.A. Harbor and Long Beach. In the future we would overnight here aboard the docked Queen Mary before then taking a launch over to Santa Catalina Island for a family holiday.

Moving on we visited Orange County, Huntington Beach and exclusive Newport Beach. Our destination was the once cozy, now virtually hard to find, but still charming town of Laguna Beach. Carrying on we stopped at San Juan Capistrano, and then continued our beach hopping by visits to San Clement, Carlsbad, Encinitas, Del Mar, stunning La Jolla, and lunch at Torrey Pines before settling in for a stay in San Diego.

San Diego enjoys the best climate in the world. Along with this, visitors have the opportunity to partake of an abundance of other high quality diversions - the unique Coronado Hotel, the world class zoo, a yacht harbor and renowned boating, fishing, and beach activities, major level sports teams, and its unique "old town" that features Mexican food and mariachi music. Did I mention the weather and the vast selection of golf courses?

Taking the inland road north from San Diego, we turned off eastward for a remarkable, eerie scenic drive over and thru the prominent hills to land on the other side at the foothill desert community of Palm Desert. We then oasis hopped our way for a stop-over in Palm Springs.

On our return through the Cajon Pass route to the Los Angeles basin, we again diverted up to the Big Bear and Arrowhead Lake Resorts atop the San Bernardino Mountains where we hiked and relaxed.

When recharged, we wound our way back down where we merged onto the immense Southern California freeway system that brought us directly to the L.A. Airport. Triumphantly we celebrated the completion of JoAnn's introductory tour by lunching at its famous geodesic global landmark.

She was exhilarated, happily exhausted, and I was pleased. We went on to spend the balance of our holiday time with a stay on the Big Island of Hawaii for recovery before making the long flight back to our home on Kwajalein.

As a quick summary review, this is an apt parallel portrayal of the many excursions we had the good fortune to have visited and similarly enjoyed over many years in the regions of Eastern Asia and New Zealand, and several countries of Southern Europe and the Mediterranean.

Traveling through life with JoAnn was a memorable, priceless, shared adventure.

RMH

.10-2014

Bonding

To select a term that best depicts the primary concern and most devoted effort extended by JoAnn toward achieving personal satisfaction over the many years after returning "home", I would choose the word bonding.

Though never being totally out of touch, and having maintained a schedule of annual visits, she had mostly lived a life consumed in work and activities far distant from her family for a period of some eleven years, which could well have caused her to have a personal feeling of remiss.

Now, having returned to her old haunts, remembered routines, and past friends, and her family of two sons, Greg and Doug, who were now married adults with families, and, especially thrilling for her, two grand-daughters, Amanda and Elizabeth, JoAnn had a lot of "bonding" work to do. Soon, Donna, her daughter would also return to re-establish her home in the Huntsville area. She was a busy lady in those first years, and then with many new friends in the settling-down years that followed. It's easy to understand the good and importance that is derived from bonding. It's not as easy to describe all the areas of occurrence. To mention a few:

1 – Old Friends
Almost immediately upon her return, JoAnn re-contacted her

old friends with whom she had shared their family building years in Athens. As best as I recall, Margaret was the leading mom, and her closest comrade from those very close and important years. They regularly met for "Southern Lady" gatherings for many, many more years.

2 – Kwaj
The first "group" that began our circles of lasting friends were the retirees from Kwajalein who lived in the area; the headquarters for the Kwajalein Island project is based on the Redstone Arsenal facility in Huntsville. Our bond with our fabulous Kwaj alumni friends has been an enduring joy and godsend.

3 – Neighbors
It was literally within days after we had acquired a likeable house and transformed it into our home, that JoAnn became involved with "her" neighbors; I had to sort of grow into the blending. Her best friend from Kwajalein, Ann moved into the neighborhood about the same time. So, along with Cindy and another Ann and a half dozen other ladies they quickly bonded into a band of shopping/lunching suffragettes. Over the years their touch of human connectivity was a comfort to behold for me, and always of great, enduring importance to JoAnn.

4 – Church
Another venerable cohort group that she courted and developed was from within the congregation at her University Baptist Church; the church ladies and their husbands. This became a bonding of deep personal fulfillment. This, and her involvements with such as Meals-on-Wheels were very satisfying and

compatible with her nature. The kindness of Pastor John Robert Burt, Maurine, and many other heroic cohorts supported her in her hours of greatest need, and sustained me during my deepest fog.

5 – OLLI

The Osher Lifetime Learning Institute established an affiliation with the University of Alabama in Huntsville in the early 1990's. The classes and activities are comprised of a well-organized collection of education-minded, on the go, retired elder citizens. JoAnn became involved in the late 1990s. Perhaps it's been said, but above all JoAnn was well-liked. I don't know if this was an inherent trait or if there is some sort of technique that can be developed into perfection, but she had it. She "dragged" me into participation via a "looney tunes" discussion class with new friends she had made. They were a fabulous group that grew and grew, along with the joy and involvement support that Olli provided us over many, many years. It was not only stimulating and enriching, but it offered JoAnn another group of fascinating ladies for her luncheon calendar.

6 – Grandchildren

JoAnn's concern for her granddaughters was obvious and enduring. She truly enjoyed her times with them. I believe that Amanda and Elizabeth found their occasions with her to be fun as well. I hope so for they will be part of their memories. I don't know what they talked about, but I hope they realize that they had a "fairy-god-mother" for a grandmother, just as I had a heaven-sent wife.

Though probably never perfect, I know that JoAnn always

tried. I took note of how she treated them differently. <u>Elizabeth</u> was younger and JoAnn began bonding with her when she was young enough to be bathed in a sink, and then over the years being involved with her in their cosmetic make-up parties, and then their dress-up parties using JoAnn's clothes. On her age 16 trip with her grandmother and aunt, she chose Disney World. <u>Amanda</u> was already active when she attended her grandmother's wedding in Florida. She too participated in the dress-up parties, but she was also of an age that involved school activities, and a Thanksgiving visit with Ray's family to Grove Park Inn in Ashville, NC. Her age 16 visit was to the spas in Sante Fe and Taos, NM. This is a mere glimpse of her many "bondings" with Amanda and Elizabeth; they were of enormous importance to JoAnn.

7 – Donna

Any need for a bond between JoAnn and Donna, her oldest child, had long been established. Nevertheless, an entire book should be written about their mother/daughter "buddy" rela-tionship. Aside from the hosting of our marriage and our fun holiday in Hawaii, I must mention my gratitude and feelings of happiness and pride whenever they schemed up and shared their adventure trips, such as those to Puerto Vallarta and Cozumel spas and New York City shows. Their special bond revealed and fully highlighted the nature, spirit and boldness of JoAnn, she always had a ready smile, maintained a zest for life, kept a steady pace, and provided an abundance of treasured memories for Donna.

JoAnn with Daughter Donna

JoAnn with Sons Douglas and Gregory

RMH
5-2015

As It So Happened

I don't recall how it all came about, but as an adventure it came together as though preordained.

Not that it was the greatest excursion on our travel card, but it was full of variety, truly impressive in grandeur, and a lot of fun. By now JoAnn and I were fully settled back home, retired and truly unfettered when somehow we were connected with "Train Holidays". It so happened many years earlier in another era, when living and traveling around out West, I had twice contemplated a trip up into the Canadian Rocky Mountains. It never came about. And then, as if by fate, we happened upon a unique gem of a tour formatted around this stunning area.

Train holidays creates unusual "three-elements-of-transport" excursions developed around railway / roadway / and water. This experience included Seattle, Victoria and Vancouver in Canada, Jasper, Lake Louise and Banff in the Rocky Mountains, followed by a cruise down the west coast from Vancouver to Mexico, Central America and on through the Panama Canal on up to Ft. Lauderdale, Florida. We disembarked in San Diego, California to rendezvous with family before returning home.

The plan was for guests to arrive in Seattle by train, or air in our case, for a city tour and overnight. We arrived even earlier to visit with Lucy, an ex-Kwaj friend who guided us through the sites, the famous fish market and space needle, and over to Victoria on Vancouver Island to take in the famous Butchart Gardens.

From Seattle, our first stop was Vancouver and a formal boarding of our train for a trip up into the great mountains to Jasper. On the ride you chat and snack while viewing the spectacular scenery from your seat in the window domed viewing cars, eat formal meals, and then entrench for the night in your sleeping car quarters. Basically you're pampered while moving along without ever lifting a finger.

In keeping with its setting, Jasper was casual, log cabin rustic with caribou wandering the grounds and streets. This was sort of our headquarters from which we round tripped South along the top of the mountains down to Banff. Along the way, seated in our large windowed tour bus, we gaped at the awesome size and variety of jutting rock peaks. We stopped at glaciers, flowing rivers, deep lake filled gorges and vast spectacular views. Banff is a smart mountain resort retreat with a stunning hotel, It offers an attractive ambiance that meets the prominence of St. Moritz, on our return back up North, we were enthralled by a reverse view of the Rockies and stopover visit at the Lake Louise resort.

Back in Jasper we boarded our train for the journey down through Kamloops to Vancouver viewing the majestic mountains and forests all the way. We toured Vancouver and then boarded our cruise ship to overnight before sailing away the next morning. Our tour mates now became out shipmates.

We were joyfully met in San Diego by Ray's sister and nephew, Carolyn and Casey. We visited over cocktails at the Hotel Del Coronado and ate once again at "our" favorite old town Mexican Restaurant.

From the moment I first saw JoAnn, my number one forte was observing her. On this trip, her joy in getting to sleep in her train bunk bed left me with the thought that the vastness of the great outdoors and forests and nature, led her to the belief that, in her mind, she was camping out. Such was JoAnn.

RMH

1 – 2014

Wine Touring, Napa Valley, CA

Luxury Ocean Cruising

Casual Caribbean Cruising

Dome Car View, Canadian Rockies

Grandma with Amanda, FL

Opryland Hotel, Nashville, TN

With Amanda & Elizabeth

Rockefeller Plaza, New York

The Alamo, San Antonio, TX

Golden Gate Bridge, S.F., CA

Santa Catalina Island, CA

Retirement from US Army Missile Command, Huntsville, AL

With the New Year comes the Rose Parade & Football

The Fun Runs

After having lived an unanticipated, remarkable island lifestyle, accented with wondrous worldly experiences for more than a decade, the time came for a return to our homeland to begin another chapter. We had no pre-set plans, but, perhaps because we had chocked up such an effortless mass of happy mileage together, our eyes were wide open with only eager anticipation. And, as always happened when with JoAnn, her employer, the U.S. government, saw to a smooth relocation back to Kwajalein headquarters in Huntsville, Alabama, USA.

And, just as I had been told by island friends, "You'll like Huntsville, Ray", I did, and so did JoAnn. She had lived her former family years before Kwajalein in Athens, a much smaller nearby town, but she was well acquainted with Huntsville and the area. The transition was seamless.

The most immediate challenge we had to face was the fact that our past life on a tiny island had been conducted within a ten minute ride on a bike, and we had re-located back into a thriving city with hills and dales, streets and highways, and an assortment of neighborhoods and business, shopping, work and service locations. All of these, and the places that offered entertainment, activities and eating, all now demanded transport and an immediate adjustment to daily life. Fortunately, this too was readily met, as was the necessity of finding and settling into a desirable, convenient, comfortable dwelling, which we turned into our home.

The next observation of our new homeland was much larger in scope and greater in challenge and opportunity. The experience of tasting the adventures offered by an unfettered lifestyle had provided us with eyes sensitive to the vast wonders of America that loomed around us.

We eagerly started our exploring in the South. First, with frequent visits to her family in near by towns, and jaunts to suggested local points of interest; rivers, lakes, waterfalls and canyons, and then, off on more expansive excursions to the more renowned highlights: Lynchburg, the home of Jack Daniels whiskey; muscle shoals and Memphis for their music history; Chattanooga, for its aquarium, unique Rock City vista and historic Civil War sites; Mammoth Caves in Kentucky; Helen in the mountains of North Georgia; and the botanical gardens, state capital, and campus of famous 'Alabama' in Tuscalusa.

Our curiosity and basic nature took us on extensive trips to important places. We checked out Atlanta, Charleston, Savannah, St. Augustine, South Beach, the Keys and Panhandle of Florida, and all of the gulf area from Destin to New Orleans and Galveston. In all, we became well acquainted with our new location.

And it was good that we did, because that's where all the fun came in. Virtually from the first days that we landed and settled into our new home, the flow of visitors began. The cast consisted of family members and past 'prior-to-Kwaj' friends from out of the area, several from as far away as California.

In an effort to welcome and entertain our mostly never been in the South, visitors, we boiled it all down to two primary, "should see" destinations, to which we developed full day and over-night tours. We christened them, 'The Fun Runs'.

Our primary 'Fun Run' was a day trip to Nashville. The drive up from Huntsville was about 90 minutes on a wondrous freeway that was an easy ride as you glided on the rolling hills and enjoyed the viewing of the scenery. This drive was never a bore or disappointment. As you round a curve, your arrival at Nashville is surprisingly sudden as it makes a grand and rather modern appearance. The city sits on a river and as you approach it from the South the road splits and encircles its central area so that you can enter from its west or east side. Downtown features museums, vintage music bars, dance halls and the original 'Grand Ole Opry' Ryman Theater. Today it also sites the NFL Titan Football Stadium.

Moving on from this unique historical area to the East edge of town, we come to the purpose of the run, the Opryland Hotel. In the earlier years a prime feature was its amusement park and roller coaster, and river boat dock for the fun of lunch and dinner dining cruises to-and-fro downtown. This area now sites a huge shopping mall and new, larger Opryland Theater. The "landmark" is now the Omni Hotel.

The treat of the run is the Hotel with its grand entry and long shop lined foyer that leads to its awesome open air five story 'indoor' arboretum with two levels of pathway viewing of its canopy of lush trees, green shrubbery and exotic floral beds. The winding paths lead to another spectacular open air, indoor area which features an array of restaurant seating areas surrounded by water pools with spectacular displays of synchronized spouting fountains.

If this is not enough, today this area connects to an expansion of the hotel into an addition of even greater dimension. Again open aired and indoors with high walls of windowed view rooms that look out at an indoors water way that surrounds an island that provides a patio tavern and boarding dock for gondola riding. The area also houses a full sized restaurant and another fountain theater.

Out return to Huntsville could be via a different freeway that takes us to Chattanooga and its unique Rock City extraordinary mountain top rock formation and spectacular, unforgettable view, or a choice that goes through Lynchberg and a guided tour of the Jack Daniels brewery. These are all memorable treats for Southerners and visitors alike.

⁂

The more distant 'fun run' not only featured a visit to another remarkable hotel, the Grove Park Inn resort; and a tour of the renowned Loire Valley inspired chateau, the Biltmore House estate, both situated in Ashville, N.C., but also, a stop-over in Gatlinburg, an idyllic fairy tale village situated on a slow moving river in Smokey Mountain Park.

These jaunts always left us feeling good and full of pride; not for the existence of such remarkable treats or for the joy of having shared them, but that we actually felt that they were our "discovery". I wonder if being selfish, smug and silly is a "sin"?

RMH
4-2015

Life With Ray

Luckily for posterity and my amusement, an iconic photo of JoAnn was taken while riding on the indoor roller coaster at the Mall of America in Minneapolis.

We were in Minnesota for a farewell gathering of her 'additional' new immediate family after attending a very rare, full Helstrom family reunion. It could be said the photo perfectly captures her reaction to what she had gotten herself into when she became involved and married to Ray while on Kwajalein. In my heart I'm sure that her new "life-with-Ray" wasn't wild or bad, it was just different.

Yet, looking back through her eyes, it must have been quite a ride in terms of unexpected frenzy and chaos. Her lifestyle of annually bouncing about on a worldly scale as a twosome would now find that pace accelerated. Though on a smaller scale, the occasions were much more frequent with a far larger cast of characters. Fortunately her Southern composure served her well. The above notable event was but one of dozens of immediate family ventures she would experience during her retirement years. The flavor of a variety of others are worthy of mention:

It wouldn't be true in its entirety to say that JoAnn's life-with-Ray began when we were both introduced to Ray's grandson, Garrett, on the morning after his birth in Pasadena, Ca.. However, it might be fitting, and possibly clever, to equate or match the celebration milestones of Garrett's early year birthdays with a few shared events that transpired when JoAnn became a major member and player in Ray's family.

❧

For instance, after the occasion of Garrett's birth, the first gathering we enjoyed with the family was a visit to Marek and Wendy's home in Bangkok. Britt was about age seven and Garrett was between 1-2. The visit was a success; Garrett had his own maid and was called the little Buddha, JoAnn rode on an elephant, and we got a reminder of the intensity of the heat and amount of people that exist in Thailand.

❧

The next rendezvous with Garrett and the family was in the Louisiana bayou area at Lafayette where they had relocated from Thailand and had acquired a home on a small river that ran through town. We began a series of visits where we toured the entire Cajun region, cruised the river on their boat to other landing spots, ate the unusual food, and became well acquainted with New Orleans. Over time Britt would become an accomplished swimmer and Garrett learned how to play. In all, this turned out to be another exotic, interesting, "foreign" place to visit.

⁘

Perhaps due to a need for a change in climate, or to re-live pleasant past adventures, Marek, Wendy, Britt, and of course Garrett, made arrangements for all of us to meet in Denver for a mountain skiing excursion up in Breckenridge, Co. We bought some clothes and rented all the necessities including a lodge with a hot tub. We faced the forces of this winter wonderland without a whiff of suffering, and braved the huge drifts and banks of snow while touring Leadville, Vail and Aspen. Marek and Wendy attacked the slopes with an exceptionally adept Britt, Garrett joined the bunny kids, and JoAnn was assigned to the experience of ski school. As a devotee in the long ago past, I gave it my best until my legs gave out. Riding snowmobiles capped off another thoroughly exhilarating family adventure.

⁘

As happens, a change in oil company job assignments returned Ray's family to California, where they located in Bakersfield. I was never enamored with this mid valley area, but it turned out well for our visits. Their home was well situated, schools were good, Britt advanced her swimming skills, Garrett continued to grow and had harvested a collection of assorted colored karate belts. He also personally received an autographed baseball from Tommy Lasorda for his participation in little league.

The treats for us were the "Ray's Family Tours"; we visited Sequoia National Park for the giant trees, went to the coast for the Hearst Castle, Santa Barbara, Solvang and Malibu. A very special outing that seemed to bring out the best in Garrett and added rose to JoAnn's cheeks and happy memories to her dreams was a family holiday on Santa Catalina Island. We spent a day aboard the docked Queen Mary before launching over the next day. Sharing fun was the purpose of our events; they never failed!

I must not forget to record another California visit that was nothing short of superlative. We ventured North from Bakersfield to a statewide swim meet near Orinda. After the event we wended on to Napa Valley for a tour visit of the renowned wineries, which included several towns and good food. Next we spent a few sophisticated days in San Francisco. Then, for the frosting of our tour, we drove down the coast to the breathtaking realm of Monterey and Carmel and Big Sur. This treasured area being old haunts to each of us, now made this opportunity to share its splendor together an even greater blessing. Marek even took us to a spectacular beach that I had never seen before.

Garrett was almost in his teens when we hit upon a fun get-together jackpot. We started this excursion by first getting the family to Huntsville. We then organized and took a comfortable drive to the

Southeast corner of Tennessee to the Ocoee River site developed for the Atlanta Olympic Games river rapid competition events. The river flows down from the North Georgia Mountains.

The entire area is a scenic wonderland that provides a spectacular outdoor experience that features a horse back riding dude ranch, cabins, chuck wagon food, rappelling wall towers, hiking in mountain gorges, visits to Alpine villages such as Helen, and tube rafting on a slower river. The highlight, of course, is the thrill of running the teeming, leaping, ferocious rapids of the boulder strewn Ocoee Olympic Games course. Marek, Wendy, Britt and gutsy JoAnn braved the challenge; only Wendy got tossed out. As she did on the 60' rappelling wall, JoAnn proudly held her own. Garrett and I drove up higher to the tube rafting facility on the slower, small rapids river. In all, this was one of the truly action filled excursions for the memory bank.

JoAnn made the flow of our remarkable life together seem normal and easy. It was always so real, proper and good, and full of fun. I severely regret never having paused to discuss with her what she thought about it all. My words have expressed my thoughts; her words would have confirmed my memories and validated the enormity of my loss.

RMH
6-2016

Casinos
(Slots & Shows)

Before revealing one of JoAnn' minor proclivities, I feel it would be beneficial for me to introduce Tom, a buddy from my high school days. The last time I saw Tom was about eight years after we had graduated. He was a sight for sore eyes, and was working as a croupier at a casino in Las Vegas. Tom was Italian and he had an unusual, impressive last name, quite possibly derived from a small coastal town located on the Mediterranean Sea in Northwest Italy, near the French border.

JoAnn and I had done a bit of travel, a good amount of which could be described as wandering. We were both blessed with the attribute for seeking out different places and seeing new things simply for entertainment and sometimes for trying out some of the activities we came across. One of these places was the casinos. Not those where there was just gambling, I mean the ones that were huge, or at least large. They aren't everywhere; they tended to be concentrated in clusters or established as special, exclusive rendezvous. Most offered stage shows as enticing attractions along with a wide assortment of gaming activities and spectacular displays of equipment. In our wandering, we came across several.

There is no doubt that they exist, but I have no recollection of our being in any casinos or doing any gambling in Hawaii or the Far East.

My remembrance of JoAnn's first involvement in casino slots and shows took place in South Lake Tahoe. We had a stopover stay in Stateline, Nevada which we used as our headquarters for a tour of the area and the lakes' fabulous scenery.

We traveled down from the mountains to the historic towns of Virginia City and Reno. I had visited the area some thirty years earlier and thought it would be an amusement for JoAnn. We toured the casinos on the renowned main street and then took in a dramatic new one on the edge of town where we saw one of the spectacular Cirque du Soleil shows. As was our way, we sampled several of the offered 'sporting' games. To be honest, we never really gambled - we were more like high-spirited 'dabblers'. Over time, JoAnn settled on 'poker slots' as her favorite.

It was back up in Stateline where the experimenting and fun began. And also where Tom entered the scene. A display bulletin had announced that the featured show in town would be The Gatlin Brothers and Roger Miller, which seemed especially fitting for our outdoorsy, rustic location. That evening, we eagerly arrived at the theater to find a long line down the sidewalk outside of the casino. Now, since this happened some thirty years ago, I can't recall the exact procedure in use for the buying of tickets, getting in line, and when everyone was told to enter, and where they sat, but here's what happened.

First, I'm not much for standing in lines. I told JoAnn to play the slots and I'd come and find her in a few minutes. I then went to the theater entry doors; talked casually with the 'guys' and asked for their 'main' man; when introduced, I told him that my friend, Tom (**last name**), from Las Vegas, said I could use his name at the clubs if I needed anything, not for comps (free tickets), but for help or a favor; I then asked him if I could get our tickets and go in before the line was released. It worked! I went and found JoAnn and life went on.

Some years later, we were in Las Vegas. Again, I had been there in the past but now it was twice as large and three times as spectacular. We were strolling up the strip after lunch and noticed a casino across the street with a long line out front. The marquee indicated they were waiting for the afternoon performance of Sigfreid and Roy. We crossed the street and went in; I found the 'main' man; and, guess what: It worked, again! This time, it was slightly different - he arranged a signal for when we should enter the theater.

When JoAnn and I had a stopover in Nice, France we visited a famous casino in Monaco. The casino is a grand, austere building overlooking a small harbor filled with million dollar yachts. Its interior is stately with the aura of Tiffany Jewelers. As an island friend had once described it, "You don't dare drop a quarter, because it would cost you a dollar to tip a floor walker who picked it up for you." At the back of the main floor there are several impressive closed doorways to private rooms where I am sure the serious games are played. JoAnn braved the slots, but I was far too intimidated to try my luck.

Another surprising treat was an evening at a casino on the island just east of Montreal, Canada. It seems that everywhere you go there's always something unexpected and interesting. And fun, also, such as our stopovers when traveling to or from Texas and finding in Mississippi, the Beau Ravage near Biloxi and Tunica just south of Memphis, Tn.

It's mandatory that I mention one other occasion in Las Vegas. The story is too long to tell here but, because it concerns a casino and incorporates all of the ingredients of slots, shows, 'main' men, Tom, and a wonderful, memorable experience for JoAnn, it's imperative. The featured show was one of Sammy Davis, Jr.'s final performances, and, due to her being petite, it involved arranging for front row seating so that she wouldn't miss a thing. Unbelievably, Tom (**Last Name**) came through again!

One final thought concerning poker slots; perhaps there is someone unaware that cruise ships are havens very similar to casinos. My main recollection of JoAnn's enamor for the lifestyle of cruising was the fun of dressing up for dinner, followed by feeling carefree and independent and enjoying the dinners themselves. And, or course, attending the nightly shows. There was also some dancing, and NOW, as I write this anecdote, my memory recalls the SLOTS!

I mentioned that we were wanderers and that we just dabbled at games. In all honesty, I really don't know if we ever won or lost; it never crossed my mind and it was never discussed. JoAnn's happiness was paramount in our togetherness.

RMH
3-2015

The Christmas Train

Along with our demand for a continuous lifestyle list of fun things to do and see, the joy JoAnn experienced when sleeping while riding aboard a train had to have some bearing on the issue, and the early December time frame was definitely another. I'm speaking here about an idea for an excursion.

The scheme we were concentrating on had to adequately serve as an appropriate entertainment we desired for a coming holiday season. The result became our Christmas Train holiday.

The plan that evolved was designed to cover new territory, provide new sights, indulge our curiosity and surprise us with some unusual and unique holiday season décor. What we blocked out and pieced together was derived from our predilection for adventure, our imagination, and a smattering of past experiences. We thought about big city outdoor decorations, and what cities would offer the most, where were they located, and how we might best transport ourselves round trip from Huntsville, AL.

The ultimate itinerary would incorporate these elements: we would stay in the East, driving in winter was out, flying was too swift and boring, and NYC window shopping, the White House Christmas Tree tour, and something foreign were priorities.

When it came to the logistics, time was never an issue; the crucial essential was timing. Everything was developed around several key reservations; the time of our White House entry pass; our transport schedule; hotel accommodations during the holidays; time for sightseeing; a squeezed in reservation at a sky top view restaurant in NYC and ticket bookings for two shows. Looking back, the challenge seems to be far too much work than it did at that time. Vigor is important; aging is a burden in life.

The ease and fun of our earlier mountain train trip brought Amtrak into the picture. It's route from New Orleans through Birmingham, Al. Washington D.C., to NYC, and then on up to Montreal, Canada put the bow of feasibility on the top of our excursion package. Moving beyond the itinerary nightmare effort that created this holiday, some of the highlights that pin the badge of success onto the breast of this concoction are worthy of revelation.

We boarded our transport train in Birmingham and after a day-over in NYC we went north along the Hudson River up to Montreal, Canada, our first city. As expected, it was cold and wintry, but surprise, the train enters Montreal underground, where you arrive into about a four-block city in full operation, and surprise, directly above the train station the lobby of our grand hotel was located. There was virtually no reason to face the cold weather outside but, of course, forget about that. We were there for the sites and lights.

Montreal was a joy; it was old and quaint, festive and "Frenchy"; it has an even older town section filled with restaurants and bistros, grand cathedrals, McGill University, and a casino on a neighboring island. The visit was stimulating.

Our return down through the Adirondack Mountains to New York was scenic. We settled in and started out at our usual pace. We had blocked in our days and nights exclusively to mid-town (this was our third visit and it was winter). Mandatory viewing were the Fifth Avenue stores and window displays, skating at Rockefeller Center and Central Park, the Plaza Hotel, the familiar delis, Sardis, P.J. Clark Pub, and a tower revolving view restaurant, Times Square, and of course, the Radio City Music Hall Rockettes Christmas production, plus the showings of "*Chicago*" and "*Smokey Joe's Café*".

We then, again boarded our train for a relaxing, patriotic visit to our Nation's Capital. The highlight was the Christmas tree and holiday tour of the White House. Possibly due to the seasonal timing, joyfully we had the entire Washington D.C. area to ourselves. Unbelievably there were no crowds. We crawled all over the capital, toured museums and art galleries, and visited all of the monuments. The trams were running, so with ease we visited the Georgetown malls, important Kennedy Center and renowned National Cathedral. Our idea for a "little holiday diversion" turned out to be a treasure of memories. Such was life with JoAnn.

The topper may have been that when we arrived in Birmingham, our car, parked all alone at the train station, was fully intact and in perfect condition. Once again, a big "thank you" to JoAnn's karma.

RMH

2-2015

And Then It Hit!

Sometimes serious things occur. And being human, my thoughts say that it's quite normal to then adorn ourselves with whatever cloak we use to cope with calamity. Mine was six years of fog. JoAnn adeptly donned her manner of complete composure. Looking back, as she faced a sudden, devastating and horrendous personal assault, her every gesture was always saintly and heroic.

As I recall, it was on the Friday of the week that we returned from a visit in California. On a normally-scheduled appointment with her doctor, his examination initiated the urgent scheduling of a second opinion appointment for the following Monday with Dr. Joe Kelly, an ovarian specialist surgeon. He immediately took charge of her case and managed her ordeal over the next three years.

This event became a hand-wringing, heart-wrenching episode that gratuitously granted the inclusion of a one and a half year period of remission. As an episode, it included immediate surgery followed by regimented treatment at a brand new cancer center, which I lovingly refer to as her alma mater. Her matriculation consisted of six-sessions of specialized chemotherapy. And then, after the return of her affliction, another six-session treatment, which was then followed by a brave, voluntary four-session experimental treatment on behalf of an effort to advance the medical treatment of ovarian cancer.

It could be said that our attendance at a memorable Kwajalein Alumni Reunion in Colorado Springs marked the end of her time of remission or the beginning of her last year of life. I accept the former and grudgingly concede the latter.

Though the ordeal was stunningly sudden, hugely serious, and enduringly long for JoAnn, through it all, her nature and persona turned the event into being simply another excursion. She was incredibly strong and truly heroic. What a remarkable lady - have I mentioned that I loved her dearly and deeply?

RMH
9-2017

At home: Dressed for an evening out.

Neighbor Friends say Happy Birthday.

The "Family" in our last year together.

At a Kwaj Reunion; Colorado Springs.

With close friends Ann and Gerry

A stop at Yosemite on an excursion.

Part IV

The Event

Weathering

Acceptance

Acknowledgment

The Music Stopped

The day was inevitable. And she, having been assigned to the care of hospice, it was humbly and patiently anticipated. We abhorred her discomfort, and for her sake it was becoming overdue. But why today? Why now, when I look upon her angelic face and plead for her agreement as I inanely utter, "We did good, didn't we?", and have her response be silently answered with a treasured, tender smile. Why, shortly after, as I held her for needed comfort, was the decision made to end our vigil? Why was this the moment she left us?

Importantly, for trauma or good, Donna, her devoted daughter, and Amanda, her beloved granddaughter, were present to forever bear witness. This was the day that the season of our joyous carnival of a life summarily closed, the midway ceased to teem, the carousel stopped its spinning, the great wheel halted its turning, and all the festivity of color and blaze of lights were dimmed. With the music silenced, our romp was over.

Gratefully, JoAnn and I had tasted a bit of the world together, and happily there were moments of time that she thoroughly enjoyed. Our experience of sharing is my strongest support as I linger on and ponder. There was a lifetime of richness in our togetherness.

When I first sighted her, she appeared to me as a precious, perky little bird that one is urged to gently hold in hand. She was small but brave and fragile, but not delicate, just vulnerable. Her kindness and understanding nature toward everyone were inherent traits that she wore like a soft, feathered cloak. She was always thoughtful, trusting, sweet, and, though rebellious over the description, infinitely good. All were part of her beauty. The photogenic wonder of our accumulated collection of worldly photos of her confirms the rest.

She was not shy. She was forever enthusiastic and full of zest. JoAnn was well liked.

I would never fault anyone for questioning why she would select someone like me to fulfill her dreams and wishes. If I had ever stopped to rationally reason my unrelenting pursuit to be the recipient of her grace, it's quite possible that I would have paused. It didn't happen. And, to be totally honest, the principle reason for her decision was due to her response to what she knew and felt was an opportunity to fulfill her deepest personal dreams. It wasn't anything instantaneous. She saw her life as it was and imaginatively came to see what it could be and came to the conclusion that, "it's my turn". My simple role was to make it happen. The wonder of her accomplishments of blossom and growth were enormously satisfying to me.

My service to a little bird was the achievement of my life.

RMH

4-2013

September 8, 2009

I am writing to confirm the conclusion of JoAnn's heroic three-year struggle with ovarian cancer.

I ask forgiveness for my lack of contact this year, I was simply unable to talk or write of it. My e-mail updates were to a short list. The last memo stated:

> With grateful thanks I am able to say,
> There was a time and place for us, &
> I honestly feel we made the most of it.,

But it really hurts to forward this ultimate message: JoAnn left us September 1 at 1:20 pm. I have enclosed an announcement and invitation concerning the time of the Memorial Service and her requested Remembrance Celebration.

In her memory, I thank you for your friendship, support, and many personal gestures of kindness that you extended toward her.

Sincerely yours,
Ray M. Helstrom

What To Say About JoAnn

Testimony of Ray Helstrom at Her
Memorial on September 12, 2009

JoAnn was beautiful; as a woman, as a mother, as a friend, and as a model person and even more so as my wife and dear, dear companion.

She radiated goodness and femininity with a carriage of innocence and total decency.

She was earnest with only thoughts of others. If she ever felt intimidated by someone, her innate instinct manifested as a concern that the other person might feel embarrassed.

I know that you, who knew her as an employee, or workmate, or as a good neighbor, or as a member of her faith or activity or luncheon group, or as a proud Kwajalein alumnus and friend, ALL hold fond memories and loving thoughts about JoAnn.

I know, too, that she was a lasting friend to many, many other wonderful people who are not present here today.

JoAnn was born and lived the early third of her life in San Antonio, Texas.

Then, as her life evolved, she spent her important family rearing days in Missouri and Athens, Alabama.

Circumstances resulted in JoAnn living another third of her personal growth years on Kwajalein atoll in the South Pacific and at her home here in Huntsville.

She made lasting friends in all of these places. There was a nobility in her touch and dealings with others.

Recently I received a memo from just such a friend. I'll read a small bit:

> "Nothing less than grace and courage would be forthcoming from JoAnn. She's always been a source of calmness and unconditional affection for me. She's my lifetime best friend; I love her like a sister."

And she then goes on to say,

> "She and my mother are the only true Southern ladies ever in my life."

This close friend is also a lady of the South.

I will speak only of my special time with JoAnn.

As a person to live, work and hang out with, in every manner of speaking, JoAnn was a consummate "neat lady".

She was fun, a good sport, a gamer, courteous, polite, proper, reliable, diligent, an attentive hostess, and a full of life, loving person.

To me, we were inseparable, so her every return home was a thrill. But her glow of satisfaction when returning from having tended children at Sunday school or on garden tours, or serving Meals-on-Wheels, or enjoyment of a luncheon with the girls, were always doubly enriching.

JoAnn had a low tolerance for disorder. Yet, due to her soft heart, at home, she tolerated a small space for me and was even more lenient toward the antics of her beloved Shih Tzu, Spritzer. They shared a strong attachment.

JoAnn was a shopper. Never so much for the buying, but for the prowling and discovery, and, of course, for the bargains.

She was always a little girl in her involvements with dressing up for occasions. She often asked for my opinion. Even when she knew I'd have one she wouldn't like.

Such sessions were a chuckle to behold and a special pleasure to be a part of.

JoAnn was open to anticipation and wonder, and curious for the revelation of new sights and entertainments.

JoAnn relished traveling - the being there and seeing things.

And later, for the 'having been there' when seeing these places or things pictured in ads and movies, or described in books.

Not for smugness, she had no smugness. She simply delighted in the adventure.

JoAnn grew and blossomed measurably for our good fortune in this regard. Our stumbling upon unanticipated structures and monuments of nature were a huge thrill for her and a huge joy to have shared them with her.

She was a fabulous partner.

Perhaps the intimacy of our small island beginning forged the closeness of our bond, for no matter how vast or strange the place, we were always content and secure in our own self contained world.

JoAnn loved her family and my family. She adored and pined for, and over, every nuance of the lives and experiences of each member.

To my mind, she was a mother to die for. So much love and concern flowed from her.

So too was her station among her multitude of friends.

Real friendship was another of her gallantries. As testified by the abundant expressions of remorse and support and love and prayers she gratefully received during her long travail.

She was humbled and very pleased by the outpouring.

Your outpouring. Thank you.

In her last days, JoAnn was seamless in her personal serenity as her body fought a massive fight.

Her strong devotion carried her lightly and in comfort as she faced her journey without fear.

As an aside that bears witness as to how she carried us all through our last 80 days vigil, let me set this scene:

After worrying and sorting out the appropriateness and fairness of a distribution of some of her coveted items to family members as keepsakes that will now forever bear her personal touch, there came a moment of more relaxed shared time.

As JoAnn held court, with family members surrounding her bed, there was happy chatter and music selections being played on a laptop, when JoAnn, in a now most angelic manner, smiled and said, "It's good to die slowly."

I can honestly state that this was never her want or wish.

But it magnificently serves as testimony to the spirit and courage, and grace and caring nature of the marvelous lady that was JoAnn.

Before JoAnn, I experienced some things, and after, with her, I became something; an attached responsive, more fully functioning human being.

Now, with a leaden heart, I'm left to ask, how does one function absent a right arm and a vision focused on a voided view?

There are profound, deeply rooted habits to be replaced.

Much as my granddaughter must have felt a loss, when, in a fit of anger, she told me, "You're not funny anymore". Our hold on innocence and precious possessions is very fragile. The strength of an abiding love and powerful memories should allow one to endure such a fracture.

This assurance would be severely tested if not for the enormous outpouring of recognition and near universal acclimation of the goodness that personified JoAnn.

Your response authenticates our treasure.

On behalf of our families and myself, once again, thank you.

Ray Helstrom

A Salute To Hospice

The seemingly serendipity, guardian-angel-guided happenings experienced while with JoAnn as my "soulmate," were again validated in the below "letter-to-the-editor."

I had seen a newspaper article on this major Hospice occasion and out of having a good feeling for their support, I called and donated for a seat.

The event was Tux and Gown. Having "outgrown" all of my formalwear, I wore a "black" sport coat and selected an outer fringe table with a yellow flower (Texas) centerpiece.

John is a big guy. He was very cordial and wore a tux. He asked if he could sit at "my" table. We ate and had a great chat. His visit was unexpected, as were his observations and revealing sensitive comments about Hospice as printed below.

The nurse is Debbie Rose who so graciously served JoAnn through her trying vigil.

YOUR VIEWS

ospice help

here were just the two of
at the table. Mr. H. and
e. About 80 years old, he
as the newcomer – his wife
ving died in September.
ver 20 years his junior, I
as the "old timer" having
lped establish Hospice of
untsville (now Hospice
mily Care) 30 years past.
We talked of his wife, their
y traveling, the enduring
nds of all Kwajalein alum-
, my dad's death last year, of
orts. He so appreciated hos-
ce and wept discretely when
eir nurse came to hug him.
e confided that if no one
se had sat st the table, he
ould have been alone with
s wife all evening.
As we shared during Hos-
ce Family Care's wonderful
)th anniversary gala, priori-
es of life seem to focus. We

briefly touched on politics but
without energy, its siren call
too petty for the Sacred Hall
of Loves Now Gone.

While driving home it reoc-
curred to me how hospice
care is such hallowed ground
when done well. I even won-
dered if this special reverence
for life could spread across
our hyper-opinionated globe
might animosities wither, ha-
treds crumble – like at the
50th anniversary reenactment
of Pickett's Charge by the
aging soldiers who actually
fought it. As the Confederates
approached the Yankee line,
they couldn't even pretend to
kill one another. They
dropped their weapons and
embraced as old friends.

Thank you Hospice Family
Care (and hospices every-
where) for your stewardship
of waning days and your example to mankind.

John D. Haley
Huntsville, 35802

This seems to be an opportune place to insert a grateful Thank You to Dr. Frank J. Kelly, the facility and staffs at Huntsville Hospital and Clearview Cancer Institute, and a nod to HudsonAlpha Institute.

RMH
12-2017

The First Entry
(Acknowledgment – Year 2010)

Hopefully none will find this entry as being too maudlin. I compose it as a message of remembrance dedicated to JoAnn with a feeling of comfort in knowing that she had a numerous number of treasured friends. It is with appreciation for this fact, and for them personally, that I record an update of the situation as it exists on the eve of the very first anniversary of her absence.

To all who had concern for JoAnn, and especially for family members, I believe with strong assurance that, with her earthly assignment completed, the positive essence of our precious collective memories will continue to maintain and sustain us.

Two conditions have initiated this diary, entry-like report: The coming date of Sept. 1, and the "put something in writing" instruction of the helpful Grief Share Program that I have re-entered this past week. Of worthy note, besides the content of its lessons, along with my state of senility, grief has granted me another excuse for my many daily failings.

Actually I'm doing well. Amazingly the world is still here - messy as ever and as rich, if you see and dwell more upon the natural, miraculous and creative. JoAnn and I tended to share this latter approach. JoAnn did, for sure.

The process of carrying on is fast approaching a full year. Looking back I recall the winter as being especially frigid and the summer as exceptionally hot. Over the year I listened to music and reminisced a lot. I weep a bit less and not as deeply as the empty hollowness of loss may be starting to fill with solace.

Friends, old and several new, have been fabulous. JoAnn's Shih Tzu, Spritzer, has been huge. And remarkably, John Banks, a once impressive, admired acquaintance, due to our shared circumstance, has become a fast buddy. Our viewpoint and humor senses are in accord, and his Type A nature maintains a full calendar for both of us.

As an experiment, or hint of progress, or possibly fear of facing a reconstruction of the last moments in a particular room, I will make a visit to California over the period of this anniversary. It will be my first venture without JoAnn and most of my family will reunite.

With that, I hope to brave it up for another full year. My hope and prayer for all is one that offers good health, brings joy, fulfills wishes, and is rich in its list of accomplishments

RMH

8 -2010

A Horse Is A Horse

(Acknowledgment – Year 2011)

There is a very high probability that I am a horse's ass. If true, I'm fully aware that it's common knowledge that there are far more of us than there are horses, so I have no feeling that it's anything unusual. Nevertheless, I confess that the reasons for my plight make me very sad.

I have never thought about myself very much and certainly not in depth. And never in a manner that was self-deprecating. However, when you lose something or someone that was valuable to you, or critically close and vital to your very being, you begin to think of things that you did that were thoughtless. Or even worse, you begin to think of things you never even thought of doing, but should have done.

It's not a pleasant picture. The fact that it's too late now doesn't relieve me of the torment.

It goes without saying that I should have bought more flowers, and of course, kissed her a lot more often, and hugged her even more. But there were other things. So many other things.

Some were small. I remember that great graphic on a souvenir t-shirt we saw when we were on Capri. She never liked t-shirts with place names. Probably to her credit, she said no to the suggestion of getting one. I should have bought one anyway and smuggled it home for her.

I should have built that archway she wanted as a decoration over the pathway in the back yard. It was one of her creative ideas and she so enjoyed working at her landscaping hobby.

I remember the afternoon when we were touring the Northern California wine country and she was interested in going to a cooking demonstration. Instead I pushed for a sit down dinner, using as an excuse that the whole family was hungry. That was unfair. She would have enjoyed the cooking class, and in truth, the real reason we were there was to have fun. She didn't sulk, but my thoughts now tell me that she must have felt unnecessary disappointment.

A couple of fun things we talked about but never really made an effort toward organizing was a visit to the Oprah Show in Chicago and a trip out West for her to view the Grand Canyon. We did seriously discuss going to Niagara Falls. I didn't make any of these happen, and I now so truly regret it.

My most heart rending, serious, and probably most destructive, even tragic screw up was the roof incident. I know it was devastating, sobering and a deeply scary experience for JoAnn. Looking back, it quite possibly dimmed the lights and lowered the curtain on the cheerful glow of our remarkable way of life.

It happened on a Monday before the Wednesday we were to take off on another always eagerly anticipated visit with Marek, Darlene and Wendy, the grandkids, Butch, and Carolyn and Spence, and another fabulous family gathering at Remeny and Bruces' little ranchette. These California trips were always full of activity, laughter, joy and love.

Foolishly I had felt compelled to climb on the roof of our house to sweep some needle debris out of the valleys. I had done this often. This time I slid sideways and broke the principle bone of my right leg. The arrival and elaborate rescue effort of the fire department personnel was a huge entertainment for the neighbors and a moment of unspeakable despair, disgust and heavy disappointment for JoAnn. Exit the trip; enter another rehab. And add another regret.

Most people who get it into their minds reach out and take a peek at whatever may be out there in the realm of curiosity, tend to develop a bucket list. JoAnn and I had one.

In no particular order, we had chatted about the Loire Valley in France, the Italian lakes with a train ride for JoAnn up in the Alps from the Matterhorn to St. Moritz, and one I kept trying to sell her on, the Taj Mahal in Agra, India with a side jaunt to Katmandu and the Himalayas.

The one at the top of the list was Scandinavia. My wish was to take a glimpse at Finland to touch the land of my ancestry on my father's side and to visit the Hermitage in St. Petersburg. For some reason, JoAnn felt very strongly toward the possibility of this trip. Partly I believe it was to balance out our viewing of Northern Europe versus the South. The reason she gave was her desire to compare the fjords of Norway with those of New Zealand.

No one will ever understand the extent of elation and depth of pride I feel when I dwell on her reasoned contemplation for visiting Norway. One would have had to have lived our travel experience from the beginning to appreciate the enormity of growth, maturity, and sense of confidence and authority she had acquired as an experienced traveler to fully comprehend the depth of knowledge and inner understanding that she revealed in her expressed reasoning.

There is little question that I was always in total denial of the threat to our togetherness. From the onset, and all through the ever so precious time of remission, and then on through the year she fought so gallantly, the contemplation of reality was too fearsome to face. Suppression was my salvation. A reverent fog has gently served me since.

Would the absence of my state of denial have been helpful to JoAnn? Would my list of regret be any shorter? I'll never really know.

RMH

8 – 2011

Three Down; Perhaps A Few To Go
(Acknowledgment – Year 2012)

General knowledge has it that incidents and events happen in threes. I'm uncertain as to the truth of this, but the use of three illustrations has always been handy when you wish to explain or convey a viewpoint. A trilogy is a common format, and three, as a number or as a method of support seems to provide conviction and stability. I really don't know why.

Thoughts of JoAnn on her rueful anniversary brought to mind that her cancer endurance was a bout of three years. Her care under hospice after release from experimental treatment lasted three months, and now, three years have passed since she left the field of play.

Also, as all of us, I am older by three years. My age is eighty-three, which is of no point and little import, except, of course, to demonstrate that I have retained sufficient faculties to have an awareness of these trivialities. Inexplicably, even after this reasonably substantial lapse of time, I still miss her the same amount. My senses are not as numb and the world is not quite as foggy, yet the hollow emptiness endures along with the heavy weight within my heart.

It seems I can't make progress to a point where our togetherness will even begin to become a memory. Or where any concept of her being in the past will commence to develop. I can't even imagine these conditions as being a matter of choice. They may evolve in time, but without my help. I need the feeling of closeness and softness that we shared. It serves as sustenance and, in truth, it provides me with enormous support. The mere absences of her presence is just about the limit of negativity that I care to endure.

JoAnn's primary trait was her innocence. Of course, she was unaware of this, which is the essence of innocence. Her personality was such that she was always pleasant, eager and full of fun, and yet, attentive and responsible in her every endeavor. She was a diligent worker and positive in her appreciation of others' efforts. Her sensitivity towards the needs and feelings of everyone bordered on angelic. She glowed with goodness and she was good to be with. My every moment with her resulted in my being an immeasurably better me. We were close.

Her curiosity and relish of exposure to new sites and experiences was contagious. I was the beneficiary of her enthusiasm in this regard. We touched a universe of joy in our ventures to an assortment of other lands and nationalities, surpassing thirty-two in all. Good fortune blessed our matrimony. There is no doubt of that.

Who could ever imagine living a life of such extreme happiness that you are totally unaware of the extent of its wealth in terms of it being unbelievable and undeserved good luck, and then, suddenly finding that you are alone with just yourself because your alter self is gone. The streak is over. God has decided it's time to test your mettle. If it happens to you, I hope you're tough.

RMH

8-2012

Rainbows For The Scrapbook
(Acknowledgement – Year 2013)

Many may withhold belief in what I say. At least as to the reality of the truth contained in the description of a couple of atmospheric sightings that I use to support a conclusion that could be made by anyone after they had experienced the witnessing of such phenomena in their life. No matter, they serve as a good summary for mine.

In this instance, I'm referring to what could probably only happen at a geographic location where conditions are properly constituted to produce viewings that I believe were unique and unusual. Specifically, when I resided and worked in the South Pacific in the Marshall Islands, I witnessed a sight while aboard what was for me an infrequent air taxi flight from Kwajalein up to its sister atoll of Roi Namur. It was on a misty day and as we approached the landing runway, I looked out from my window and at first saw a double rainbow, which then suddenly developed and emerged to become a triple rainbow. I was in awe, and then mystified, and then delighted, and finally pleased and smug. I don't know why. Probably because I thought this was rare and that I had been exclusively granted something special. There were only a few on the plane and it was never mentioned. I didn't ask the pilots if they saw it. The incident was my personal, private keepsake.

The only reason I mention this now is because there is more. My eyewitness treasure was never trotted out for discussion in terms of comparison, even to myself, and never in any manner of thought as to being surpassed. Then, one day I was riding my bike on the oceanside road to the northern tip of our island. I can't recall for what purpose. Once again it was on a squally, misty day. I looked seaward, and there was another phenomenon.

I stopped riding and got off of my bike and stared intently to be absolutely certain. After more than a long moment of absorption, it thoroughly registered that I was witnessing a quadruple rainbow. Was this possible – four rainbows stacked in ever larger arcs. They lasted for as long as a fleeting visit and then they vanished in unison. There are no other known witnesses. Again, as a perceived experience, this is personal and private and has always remained as such.

So why bring it up? Why even mention a quirky keepsake tale that could, at best, be read and considered ridiculous and absolutely of no importance? I have no answer, except to mention a line sung by Roy Orbison in the song, "It's Over". The words are to the affect that, "You won't be seeing rainbows anymore". In taking the song in its full truthfulness, it came to me that the verse, so heartfelt, heavy and final, probably got it right, and that I was luckier than most in those I got to see.

(An acknowledgment that my life with JoAnn is past)

RMH

8 -2013

Perhaps It's Simply Life
(Acknowledgment – Year 2014)

Time is dutifully earning another testament to its reputed prowess for cushioning and easing the serious pangs of life. I'm progressing well and earnestly wish the same support for you when and if you have such a need.

As my awareness approached the anniversary of possibly the most horrendous date in my life, certainly the one that has emerged as the heaviest in hurt and remembrance, I am once again urged to express an appropriate thought and salute in memory of JoAnn. Not as a gesture, but as a privilege and duty. For me, this personal emotional effort has replaced the annual contact that was normally reserved for December.

This year, the addition of a similar experience at this approximate date one year ago, gives further importance to the deed. The loss of JoAnn on the date of September 1 was joined last year in the close timing to her date by the abrupt loss of a close friend, John Banks, on the 10th.

Any summary of my grievance life over the past half decade, would reveal one experience as being extremely major in importance. Thanks to John, that would be the extraordinary support and friendship that developed between John and myself. As fate decreed, he suffered the loss of his beloved wife Konny four months after my loss of JoAnn.

Suddenly we shared and faced a similar circumstance and I'm grateful to say, that with his fortitude and resolved we fared well. For me it's a toss up between John and Spritzer as to who contributed the most to the cause of perseverance during these past five survival years.

Of course, being a survivor is a gift of major proportion and importance. And just as grief is a product of survival, the time of grievance, beyond its task of self preservation, also provides an opportunity for serious reflection. Not to inquire as to why, but to dwell upon that which in the past had worth and then acknowledge it with sincere gratitude. This moment presents such a reflection regarding my life with JoAnn; with a nod to Kenny Rogers and a salute to Sammy Davis, Jr., I paraphrase a few appreciated words by Dorff and Panzer:

Through the years,

> you never let me down you turned my life around.
> The sweetest days I found, I found with you,
> through the years.

Through the years,

> I never had a doubt, we'd always work things out,
> and I learned what life's about, by loving you
> through the years.

Those Gratifying, Treasured Years

RMH

8-2014

The Enduring Storm
(Acknowledgment – Year 2015)

When announced, it was like being struck by a bewildering irresistible force. It arrived with a directive that I was to fully witness a merciless, cancerous onslaught upon the dearest object in my life. Without awareness, I was instantly enveloped in a smothering fog that would come to seem unending. There were torrential gusts of alarm and terror, but mostly there was just a steady state of numbness. It would be a half dozen years before there was any sense of an ebb.

Unlike the afternoon on Milford Sound in New Zealand, where we experienced the stimulation of a rare ferocious rain storm and I found myself literally leaping about the ship vigorously trying to fully embrace and absorb each gust to maximize the thrill of the entire exhilarating event, on this horrendous journey, I walked soberly, or simply stood stolidly, through it all. I was tethered to my post as merely the husband, assigned to be an accepted spectator. Hopefully my reactive behavior to an abundance of tightly wrapped moments of concern and sorrow were stoic and manly. I really don't recall.

From this advantageous position, I proudly observed and absorbed the astonishing facial and complimentary verbal expressions offered by her most crucial and qualified visitors: Dr. Zaheer Kahn, Pastor Bobbi

Burt, and Debbie Rose, her hospice care nurse. In their eyes and words she was more than stately and calmly accepting of her plight, she was saintly in her reverence. Her bravery and composure carried us all, through it all.

Within the three-year span when she was dying, she was granted about one-and-a-half years of remission. At these precious times, life was nearly normal - normal in the sense of our lifestyle, which was always full, rather active, and enjoyable. JoAnn made shopping for wigs somewhat of a treat. We went to Kwaj parties, theater events, movie and dinner dates, and even traveled a bit. An important trip was out to California for my brother Lyle's service and a gathering of our immediate family. We met with some old friends and again visited Yosemite and Sequoia National Parks. Another very important gathering was a Kwajalein reunion at Colorado Springs, Colorado, where JoAnn had an enriching visit with so many friends from our long ago past ten years of unique island life.

My state of heavy fog persisted for some six years, and now, some five-and-a-half years after she left us, it still remains. It began to recede about two-and-a-half years ago. It doesn't seem to gloom up a nice day as it once did.

Now, in a major way, this lifting fog and my fading past are dominant elements in my life. And, to be frank, I refuse to allow either of them to completely vanish. I'm sort of used to them; not for their comfort, it's just that they offer a basic sense of familiarity. They have morphed into a chamber of calming support that hopefully will never leave.

RMH
8-2015

Reminiscing
(Acknowledgment – Year 2016)

No one has had the temerity to ask if I still dwell on JoAnn. If they did, I'd have to confess that I'm not really sure I'd call it dwelling, but I do still think of her often. Actually, a lot. I still feel her presence as it influences the conduct of my personal behavior, which is a very good thing.

Whether proper, or good, or bad it wouldn't be a problem for me if someone brought up the subject, even though it's hard to believe that six-and-a-half years have passed since the clock started running.

There is one peculiar thing that has been happening lately that I don't mind mentioning. It's something out in left field as far as being what I see as being part of my lifestyle experience and nature. It has to do with country music. I don't know much about country music. I've always been into pop music, show tunes, songs by certain personalities, and widely appreciated semi-classical stuff.

I don't recall music of any genre when I was a child in upper Minnesota. I do remember as a teenager peeking into a Bob Wills Event to watch a gathering of dancing adults. I remember a recording of "Make The World Go Away" by Eddy Arnold and seeing Dolly Parton once when I was changing planes at the Dallas Airport. Over the years there were a ton of popular songs by people who were famous, many who became legends: Johnny Cash, Willie Nelson, the Bakersfield and Nashville guys and gals, and other Texans, and Hank Williams, and even Elvis in a way.

The biggest impact country music made on me, came about when I was younger, way back, back in the fifties. My friend Dick Terrazas and I were driving in Mexico heading north toward Juarez / El Paso after we had spent over a month touring sites, visiting his relatives and seeing his patron saint, who he thanked at the Cathedral in Mexico City for watching over him during his stint in the Korean War.

When we got within range near the border, the first American music we heard on the car radio was a country song. It went something like, "_she was looking back to see, if I was looking back to see_". I'm not exactly certain of the words, but they were in American English and definitely country, and we were, for sure, approaching home.

Getting back to whether I ever reminisce about JoAnn and our time together, there is a refrain that has been humming in my head lately. It doesn't disrupt or bother me; it's actually rather comforting. But it's country, and that seems irrational and odd. It's the Kris Kristofferson song probably best sung by Ray Price, "For The Good Times". I find it very fitting, and gentle and soft and sweet.

RMH

8-2016

The End

Due to its expression of love, devotion and remorse, I strongly feel that "The Long Weekend" deserves a place in "From The Collection – JoAnn".

A recent re-reading of this spontaneous lyric left me humbled and lightly dampened by the moisture of a mist that emanates from the spray that is cast off from the waterfall of achievement that must immerse true artists when they have a feeling of satisfaction over and about a favorable effort.

My humble satisfaction over "The Long Weekend" is expressed with an apologetic nod to the inspiration most assuredly sensed by Eugene Field for his epic achievement of "Little Boy Blue".

RMH

The Long Weekend

Monday morning is far too early to assess what occurred this weekend, and based on past experience, I'm in no hurry. I have not taken an inventory nor gathered things up. I know he's gone, and I am sensitive to small jolts when I casually pass and notice anything of his.

Such things as his watch-post bed/lounge and chew blanket in front of the bar where he had a view of the front porch all the way to the street; or his dining bowls on the floor in the laundry room off the kitchen; and especially of his covered step-up onto our bed where his 'hotel' bath mat draped pillow and two best friends are situated. I even felt a twinge when I noticed his larder of canned goods and nibbles in the pantry.

My imagination is already showing him trotting out to locate the exact, proper place to do his business. He was always extraordinarily polite in seeking privacy for his 'rompo'. He was a bundle of chuckle. Whether he was going or coming, with his furry little legs, his walk was exceptionally adorable. He had attractive black and white markings, with a normal Shih Tzu body and face. I never tired of the mournful look in his deep black eyes when he pleaded the importance of the immediate desire he wanted you to perform in his behalf.

Spitzer was very devoted to his two friends. They were stuffed toys. Out of a whole tub full, they were the chosen ones. 'Froggy' was probably selected, not for his color or shape, but for his four skinny legs. Shih Tzu's have no grasping jaws or fangs. Their teeth are fish-like so they tend to nip and tug. Froggy was a good size and weight to drag around. 'Shaky' came to be even better. He was one of his first and had been a small, soft bear. He was now just a rag. All of his stuffing had long ago been shaken out of him and hence he was christened for the many ferocious battle tussles he endured when Spritzer was young.

The necessary decision of closure to our incredible, life-supporting relationship was rendered only 48 hours ago. Thus, the full realization hasn't been remotely absorbed, nor even been given a thought as to being dealt with.

There is much to digest. Being JoAnn's dog, he was family and the roots run deep. There is much adjustment to be formulated with no haste required. And I am in no hurry.

RMH

6-2015

An acknowledgment of the final farewell made on Saturday at 8:30 AM.

Author's Page

The author, Ray Helstrom, views himself as just another American who has lived most of his life in the 20th century. He attributes his long and fortuitous life to the rigors of a childhood on the iron range of Northern Minnesota; his WWII teen years in a bay area Navy base town in No. California; and his vital service and college youth years in So. California, as were his important family rearing and fullfiling marketing/ management career years. His charmed adventure years with JoAnn and now reminiscing years have been blessed and well spent in the rocket city of Huntsville in Northern Alabama.